The English Coalition Conference: Democracy through Language

The English Coalition Conference: Democracy through Language

Edited by

Richard Lloyd-Jones
University of Iowa

Andrea A. Lunsford
The Ohio State University

National Council of Teachers of English
1111 Kenyon Road, Urbana, Illinois 61801

Modern Language Association
10 Astor Place, New York, New York 10003

NCTE Editorial Board: Donald R. Gallo, Raymond Rodrigues, Dorothy Strickland, Brooke Workman, Charles Suhor, *ex officio*, Michael Spooner, *ex officio*

NCTE Staff Editor: Michelle Sanden Johlas

Cover Design: Michael J. Getz

Interior Design: Tom Kovacs for TGK Design

NCTE Stock Number 13818

It is the policy of NCTE in its journals and other publications to provide a forum for the open discussion of ideas concerning the content and the teaching of English and the language arts. Publicity accorded to any particular point of view does not imply endorsement by the Executive Committee, the Board of Directors, or the membership at large, except in announcements of policy where such endorsement is clearly specified.

Library of Congress Cataloging-in-Publication Data

English Coalition Conference (1987 : Wye Plantation)
    The English Coalition Conference : democracy through language /
edited by Richard Lloyd-Jones, Andrea A. Lunsford.
      p.   cm.
    Bibliography: p.
    ISBN 0-8141-1381-8
    1. English philology—Study and teaching—United States—
Congresses. 2. Language arts—United States—Congresses.
I. Lloyd-Jones, Richard, 1927- II. Lunsford, Andrea A., 1942-
III. Title.
PE1068.U5E49 1987
428'.007'073—dc19   88-36832
                                                     CIP

Contents

Foreword

I must confess that as I traveled, alone, toward a three-week conference to be held at an unknown "plantation" miles from nowhere, a conference with fifty-nine other English teachers, my heart did not exactly leap up in anticipation. It is not my notion of the ideal use of summertime to spend three weeks conferring about anything with anybody — especially if, as seemed likely, we would sit listening to lectures. The truth is that I was cursing myself for having let Phyllis Franklin, of the Modern Language Association, and Jane Christensen, of the National Council of Teachers of English, talk me into it. Three weeks! Not just three weeks with weekends off, but twenty-one solid consecutive working days — and no wives or husbands allowed! English teachers! Curriculum — that subject of all subjects that attracts the most clichés per conference-hour! "You could not pay me enough," I found myself muttering on the plane, "even if the subject raised the possibility of genuinely new results — and here I am, having 'volunteered' to be bored silly for three weeks, for nothing but board and room!"

Am I even an English teacher, I was asking myself, in any of the senses *they'll* have in mind? I teach "the humanities," I teach "rhetoric," I teach "literary criticism." But two-thirds of *them* will be elementary and high school teachers. Now, of course, I love elementary and high school teachers. My grandfather was one, my mother was one, my daughter has been one. Two cousins, one niece, and one nephew now are schoolteachers. Indeed, I have always said that "pre-higher-education" teachers are more important that "higher." No doubt it would be profitable to meet with some of them for a few days — letting them know, perhaps, of just how much we all appreciate what they do for us, and how much we sympathize with the circumstances in which they work. But three weeks!

Obviously I wouldn't be writing this foreword if my fears had proved justified. The time spent at Wye Plantation proved to be the most profitable conferring-time I'd ever spent — more profitable and exhilarating than the weeks spent at the Dartmouth Conference on a similar subject twenty years before, even more profitable than the staff meetings I've shared each year with colleagues assigned to a given freshman course. It's in the nature of the case that neither this foreword nor the report that follows can give more than a pale shadow of why that was so. The heart of any prolonged and unique experience escapes reporter's language.

This report is written in the hope of addressing two audiences that are often thought to be antithetical: our colleagues in "English" (who travel under many different names: language arts, communications studies, media studies, linguistics, composition, rhetoric, and so on) and the great public on whose support we all finally depend. Too much official talk lately has suggested a great chasm between the two groups. "We representatives of the educated public, we government officials and business executives, know exactly what you teachers should teach and why; and we accuse you of ignorance, cowardice, laziness, and greed." "We teachers know that you public complainers haven't a clue about the actual conditions under which we work; you have never faced children of indifferent or hostile parents; you have never tried, as many of us must do, to teach reading and writing to 150 or more students each week. And you ignore our successes and exaggerate our failures."

At the conference we soon grew beyond such reductive polarities. Perhaps we would have done so even sooner had we not been presented, in the very first session, with a self-styled spokesman for "the public" who seemed to tout a kind of training we all mistrusted. An official of the Department of Education gave the opening address and charged us to join a grand national repudiation of the "skills movement," in the name of new discoveries about the importance of information. Relying on E. D. Hirsch, Jr.'s *Cultural Literacy: What Every American Needs to Know* as his scriptural text for the day, the official charged us either to embrace Hirsch's list of nearly 5,000 "cultural literacy" terms, or to come up with a list of our own.

I've never seen an audience more effectively united by one hour-long speech. We all knew that whatever else we might want to say to each other, we must repudiate that spokesman's narrow, misinformed, programmatic vision of ourselves, our history, and our charges. To be asked to impart bits of isolated information, to be asked even to think about that kind of goal in isolation from all the difficulties and complexities every teacher faces, simply trivialized the work we all do and love. Whether we were thinking of graduate students or of first graders, whether we had light teaching loads or heavy, whether we taught honors sections or remedial sections, whether our training was in linguistics, language arts, media studies, or critical theory, we knew that the last thing American education needs is one more collection of inert information, a nostrum to be poured raw into minds not actively engaged in reading, thinking, writing, and talking. Not only did we believe that abstracted lists of terms would not motivate our students to become spontaneous learners; we were sure that they would increase the tendency of too many of our schools to kill whatever spontaneity the children bring when they enter school. (This is not the place to discuss the growing controversy over Hirsch's book; a good introduction to the issues can be found in a special collection, *Profession 1988*, published by the Modern Language Association. Nor can I do justice here to our sustained probing of just how America might improve the circumstances under which too many teachers must work — circumstances that no amount of tinkering with lists to be learned will remedy.)

Though that speech (and one that followed a day or two later by Hirsch himself) had the virtue of pulling us together, it did deflect us, initially, into a good deal of lamentation about indifference and hostility in our various "constituencies." (I was repeatedly shocked by accounts of the obstacles serious high school teachers encounter daily.) But we soon got that out of our systems and settled down to the harder work of discovering whether, in addition to a common enemy, we could find common goals that applied to all levels of teaching, from the elementary years through the doctoral level. Could those university professors whose immediate thinking was reported in talk of "paradigm shifts" and "post-structuralism" meet those elementary teachers who felt that their teaching lives were corrupted by "sequencing" and "basal readers"? And could any program we might agree on make sense to a public alarmed by the "decline of standards" and the "neglect of the classics"? I think that most of us were surprised, as the days passed, to discover not only that we did share a mission, but that it was one we believed most of our "publics" would also embrace, *if* they could only take part in our kind of extended discussion about the teaching and learning requirements in a society like ours.

In short, we finally hit upon a truth that was by no means self-evident at the beginning: If you put committed English teachers together — those who are willing to spend as much as three weeks on the subject without being paid for it — and ask them to hammer out, in writing, the goals and methods they are most committed to; if you do not lecture them but spend the time in give-and-take discussion about their experiences and hopes and fears; and if you do not fix them to an agenda preestablished by some national organization or foundation — *if*, in short, you can run a conference like the one reported on here, you will find that they in fact share not just a profession with a set of assumptions and prejudices, but a *vocation*, a *calling*, a *commitment*.

If that commitment could be summarized by any one participant's statement, we would not have needed the conference in the first place. My way of putting it, added now to the variety you will find throughout this book, is that we are in this curious profession because we see "teaching English" as the best way we know of "enfranchising," "liberating," "enabling," "empowering" those who will make our future. We are all struggling — most of us paid less than we would be paid in other jobs, many of us working under intolerable conditions — to lead our students to "take responsibility for their own meanings." We hope that those we teach will become "self-starters," independent readers, thinkers, writers, and speakers: critical, active participants in a complex verbal culture, educated to do something more than spew back the floods of words that threaten to drown us all. As the report of the college section says, we seek to prepare students, whatever their ages, "who are active learners and who are able to reflect critically on their own learning. . . . In an information age, citizens need to make meaning — rather than merely consume information."

Active learners, not passive receivers: such language obviously is not brand new in our educational history. But the echoes in that language of John Dewey and other "progressive" theorists should not lead any reader to see us, as some of our critics have suggested, as falling back into the tired formula, "Teach the child, not the subject." To do so would be to engage in precisely the kind of polar thinking that has plagued too much recent criticism of the schools. We do not choose between "the child" and this or that ideal "subject." We choose subjects which, by their nature, if taught properly, will lead the child eagerly through increasingly independent steps toward full adult, self-sustained learning.

Obviously there was nothing radically new in this enterprise we discovered together: If we had not already been to some degree engaged in it, we could not have discovered our commonality at Wye. What was new was our having enough time together — three weeks soon began to look too short! — to get beyond our stereotypes, to listen to each other, to try to understand and fail to understand and then try again.

How did our astonishing agreement come about? The full story will never emerge from any one account, because each of us came with different prejudices and left with a different sense of what could and should be done back home. (Peter Elbow is now writing another book that will fill in more details.) But since I consider the process of the conference at least as important as our final recommendations, I should like to underline the special intensity of our daily labors. Morning, noon, and night, weekdays and weekends, we sorted through our differences of vocabulary, and we thus *had time* to move beyond superficial misunderstandings. Part of each day we spent with those who customarily taught on our own "level," whether elementary, secondary, or college. (I chose to meet with the secondary teachers, in the mistaken notion that I already knew what my college-level colleagues would have to say.) But we also met each day in scrambled groups, trying to distinguish those disagreements that were substantive from those that sprang from mere differences in vocabulary.

As we did so, we found that our own "learning problems" resembled those of our students back home. Though we came into each session thinking of ourselves as open-minded "listeners," most of us proved to be astonishingly resistant to taking in what the others really had in mind. Just like our students, we could not grasp on first hearing any concept that was the least bit different from what we had embraced before. And like our students, we discovered that a given phrasing revealed new depths on a second and third encounter. For example, toward the end of one morning's discussion in the secondary group, we came to enthusiastic unanimity on the question of what kind of active learner our high school classes should foster — only to have a colleague point out that our notes from the *previous* session had reported precisely the same conclusion, only in slightly different language. We had "learned" it once, then in a sense forgot it by the next day, only to "learn" it again, but at a deeper level. In short, our own learning illustrated just why our students show so much resistance to learning: like theirs, it was inevitably "recursive," spiraling, requiring repetition after repetition, as concepts that were initially only words, even repugnant words, deepened into intelligible concepts.

Reflecting on what our uniquely prolonged experience means should help readers to think about just how this report might best be read and used. It has been written by many teachers, each of them to some degree employing terms that may to other teachers carry misleading connotations. When I have shown certain sections to colleagues, I have been shocked by their readiness to leap into quite misleading inferences about what this or that recommendation means. The only antidote to such misreadings will be, first, to read the whole report before concluding what any one part "really means," and then to do some rereading, asking just what might be implied for "my teaching life" by what we recommend. Again and again, in correspondence since the gathering, I have been told by my new acquaintances from the conference, "My teaching this year has been radically improved by what we said to each other at Wye." It may be too much to expect that effect from reading any book, but that is, of course, one result we hope for.

That result is least likely to occur, in my own view, if well-meaning readers try to impose our conclusions on their colleagues as hard-and-fast truths. All of our recommendations are interpretable in diverse ways, good and bad. Each of them could be corrupted, for example, by any administrator who decided to impose it on teachers who had no chance to think it through in relation to local circumstances. Again and again at the conference, teachers reported that whenever they had been empowered, locally, to work together to decide what the curriculum should be *in their circumstances,* morale was transformed and student performance improved remarkably. In contrast, whenever goals and methods were imposed from the top, without full and open sharing of experience, the results were meager or even harmful. Thus, the best outcome for this report would be the provision of conferences and workshops as much like ours as possible: "mini-coalitions" that would, like ours, allow for a genuine digging beneath surfaces to determine just how, given the teachers and students and parents and administrators and physical plants available *here and now,* we might turn passive or hostile or complacent children toward lifetimes of active learning.

After all, it is only when we teachers engage in reflection on what we want to learn and why, only when we "take responsibility for our own meanings," that we become models of what we want our students to become. Only if we lead our students to take such active responsibility will they become full participants in the political and cultural life they will meet after they leave our care.

Wayne C. Booth
University of Chicago

Acknowledgments

The report that follows represents a most remarkable collaborative effort. In every important sense, the authors of this report are the sixty teachers who gathered at the Wye Plantation in the summer of 1987 (see Appendix A). The substance of what follows comes from them; we and our hardworking coalition editorial committee have only attempted to convey that substance clearly and accurately. To that committee and to all participants in the Coalition Conference, then, we are profoundly grateful. In addition, we are indebted to Gerald Nelms and Beverly Bruck, both of whom worked cheerfully and tirelessly on the preparation of this manuscript.

Richard Lloyd-Jones
Andrea A. Lunsford

Participating Associations

The professional associations that together form the English Coalition are:

ADE	Association of Departments of English
CEA	College English Association
CLA	College Language Association
CSSEDC	Conference of Secondary School English Department Chairs
CCCC	Conference on College Composition and Communication
CEE	Conference on English Education
MLA	Modern Language Association
NCTE	National Council of Teachers of English

Individuals who attended the Coalition Conference are listed in Appendix A, page 67.

Abbreviations

In addition to the abbreviations for the associations which form the English Coalition (see page xiv), this volume uses the following abbreviations in place of the full names of these programs and professional organizations.

ACTFL	American Council on the Teaching of Foreign Language
ADFL	Association of Departments of Foreign Language
EFL	English as a Foreign Language
ENL	English as a Native Language
ESL	English as a Second Language
IATESOL	International Association of Teachers of English to Speakers of Other Languages
IRA	International Reading Association
NAEP	National Assessment of Educational Progress
NEH	National Endowment for the Humanities
TESOL	Teachers of English to Speakers of Other Languages

Introduction

What does it mean to be a teacher of English, from kindergarten through graduate school? What common challenges unite us? What issues divide us? During July 1987, a coalition of English associations sponsored a conference to consider such questions and to chart directions for the study of English into the twenty-first century. A complete file of their exploratory answers and deliberations — of all materials produced before and during the conference — is stored at the offices of the coalition members and of the various granting agencies. Many of the participants drew on these materials to prepare essays, articles, speeches, and news items following the conference, and Peter Elbow is at work on his reflections on the conference, a volume which will be published by the Modern Language Association in late 1989. In addition, a collection of essays titled *Stories to Grow On: Demonstrations of Language Learning in K–8 Classrooms* (Heinemann, 1988) has been developed by the participants of the elementary strand and edited by Julie Jensen.

To date, however, no brief, concise report of the Coalition Conference has been available. The document before you, therefore, aims to fill this gap by presenting the major conclusions reached by conference participants about the teaching of English. This introductory section provides background information about the conference; the second section provides edited versions of position papers adopted, in principle, by conference participants; the third section includes some sketches designed to illustrate the problems and opportunities facing English studies; and the appendixes offer various details of record — participants, bibliographies, and schedules.

The Coalition Conference grew from seeds planted by representatives of eight professional associations concerned with teaching English in the United States. The officers and staff members of six of these organizations — the Association of Departments of English (ADE), the College English Association (CEA), the College Language Association (CLA), the Conference on College Composition and Communication (CCCC), the Modern Language Association (MLA), and the National Council of Teachers of English (NCTE) — met for the first time at the

1982 MLA convention to discuss subjects of general interest. Although the associations represented different constituencies within the field and were not, for the most part, accustomed to talking with one another, so urgent were their common concerns that they agreed to continue meeting after their annual conventions. Eventually, they decided to form a coalition, which the Conference on English Education (CEE) and the Conference of Secondary School English Department Chairs (CSSEDC) later joined.

While the ad hoc meetings held after conventions identified many problems, they left precious little time to consider implications. And since the associations often sent different people as representatives, the meetings lacked continuity. Under these shifting circumstances, discussions of even the same topic varied from meeting to meeting. But the educational reform movement provided a useful focus for conversation, which became increasingly purposeful as association representatives talked about a constructive response to the criticisms of the schools that were appearing with increasing frequency. The group concluded that more time was needed to explore this topic than was available at the end of a national convention. Thus, with the support of the Exxon Education and Rockefeller foundations, they arranged for a longer meeting.

The coalition met for several days in 1984 at NCTE headquarters in Urbana, Illinois, to hammer out a general statement that might be helpful to those interested in educational reform. (The statement is included as Appendix E.) At this meeting, participants became painfully aware of differences on exactly what should be taught and on how English teachers might respond to changing student interests and needs. In time, this recognition led to plans for a longer conference, one that would allow a larger group of teachers and scholars to conduct a more thorough consideration of the issues. Twenty years before, the Anglo-American conference had convened at Dartmouth, paving the way for major effects on teaching in the schools and in colleges and universities. Since that meeting, changes — in the field, in the schools, in society, and in the student population — had led almost everywhere to new demands on English teachers and, here and there, to modifications in the teaching of English, about which there was little consensus. Coalition members hoped that a national conference would encourage a consensus on some issues and identify areas of disagreement on others.

In response to a proposal prepared by a committee of the coalition and then presented and administered on its behalf by MLA, the Andrew W. Mellon and Rockefeller foundations agreed to fund the conference. Additional support came from the Exxon Education Foundation and the National Endowment for the Humanities. The sponsoring coalition members also contributed money and people to the task.

Unlike the Dartmouth Conference, which was attended primarily by college and university professors, the Coalition Conference brought together teachers from all levels of schooling. Each of the coalition associations shared in the responsibility of selecting the representatives who attended the conference. Coalition members also shared in the general planning of the conference, although they asked a small steering committee to work out the details and make the final arrangements. During the planning period, the steering committee met with the larger coalition group at the end of association conventions to report the committee's progress and to seek advice.

After years of planning, sixty teachers of English gathered from July 6 to 26, 1987, in rural solitude at the Aspen Institute's Wye Plantation in Maryland. As a whole or in subgroups, they met mornings, afternoons, and some evenings for lectures, discussions, reports, and demonstrations. Three subgroupings of all participants represented the level of the students being taught — elementary, secondary, or college. Three more groupings represented a systematic mixing of all participants, and those groups were reconstituted each week. For all meals, participants dined together graciously, even elegantly, at tables of eight people, all constantly shifting to encourage the spread of ideas and acquaintanceship. Between such assemblies, the teachers read, exercised, used word processors, and disseminated the results among themselves to the extent of wearing out three photocopying machines. The wide range of backgrounds and perspectives represented by people participating in the conference assured a thorough hearing of many conflicting views.

The conference program opened by addressing the changes that had taken place in students, curriculum, the school environment, and the larger community over the past ten to fifteen years. Participants then considered what they thought students should achieve in their formal study of language, writing, and literature; impediments to learning; cultural literacy; and the influence of television and other media. Subsequent discussion focused first on the study of language, then on the practices of oral and written composition, and finally on reading in general and on reading literature in particular. The conference concluded by examining the education of teachers at all levels. A skeletal outline of the plan is included as Appendix B, but the topics did not sort out as neatly as the plan, and conference participants were increasingly concerned with the relations among the topics. The steering committee met regularly during the conference and adjusted the program and schedule as necessary.

The theme "Democracy through Language" emerged as a result of the discussions, not as part of the plan. Conference participants confirmed the importance of the humanities generally and the specific value of English studies in the education of citizens who live in a democratic and increasingly complex information society. They noted:

> Unless students know how to read and write, they will not be able to assimilate, evaluate, and control the immense amount of knowledge and the large number of messages produced every day. The development of new media similarly requires of citizens an enhanced ability to use different ways of reading and writing, and language arts instruction has an important role to play here as well.

Making literacy a possibility for all students became a priority, and the group concluded that the interactive classroom described later in this introduction provides the best environment for achieving this goal.

Two other related goals also grew out of the group's emphasis on the social value of English studies: encouraging students to articulate their own points of view, and encouraging them to respect different perspectives. Conference participants agreed that:

> Citizens of a democracy must be able to appreciate diversity even as they advocate their own beliefs about what is good and true. Teaching students how and why different ways of reading can find different meanings in the same text can provide important experience in understanding and appreciating opposing perspectives. Learning about the many different kinds of writing and ways of thinking which are the subject matter of the language arts curriculum can expand the capacity of students to imagine and value worlds other than their own. The ability to communicate their views in oral and written form and to listen with comprehension to the views of others is also indispensable to citizens in a democratic society, and enhancing this ability is a major aim of language arts education.

Achieving these goals, conference participants decided, called for a fresh view of the field. For many years, English teachers at all levels of schooling have thought of English studies as a tripod, one of whose legs was language, another writing, and the third literature. Though the usefulness of this metaphor has been questioned over the years, it has remained influential, focusing attention necessarily on subject matter, on the objects scholars and critics read and study, and on the thing — language — out of which those objects are made. Such a metaphor does not specify classroom context, and it leaves open or blank the roles of both teachers and students. It seems fair to say that when people filled in these blanks, they were likely to see teachers acting as givers of knowledge, which students receive — more or less passively.

Though unarticulated as such, the tripod conception of English studies clearly influenced the initial division of the conference program into segments on language, writing, and the study of literature, even though during the planning process, representatives from the elementary and secondary schools expressed dissatisfaction with such an arrangement. By the end of the conference, however, the tripod and its presumption of an untroubled transmission of expertise from teacher to pupil had faded, and a more interactive, learning-centered view of English studies had emerged. With the advantage of hindsight, one might say that conference participants took the tripod, the content of English studies, for granted (or almost for granted) and concentrated on filling in what the old metaphor left out.

First, conference participants saw English studies as including a broader range of activities than the tripod suggests and talked about the English teacher's need to foster student learning in reading, writing, interpreting, speaking, and listening. They thought that encouragement of these abilities, which the college strand called the "arts of language," should continue throughout a student's education — from the elementary school to the university — developing in a recursive fashion so that the more advanced students (and their teachers along with them) would keep returning to first questions, but from progressively more sophisticated perspectives and with continually expanding bases of knowledge. Viewing English studies as a continuum from the earliest grades through undergraduate study made it easy for participants to use the term *language arts* interchangeably with *English studies*. During the conference and in this report, these terms are used synonymously and refer to the same sets of abilities.

Second, conference participants viewed the formal, school study of English as only one place where people learn to use and understand their language. In this view, schools provide a special place — and a critical opportunity — for students to continue a process that begins outside school with parents, other adults, and peers, and goes on both outside and in school. The sensitive integration of what students study formally with what they bring to the classroom from outside it was considered desirable for all students, but particularly valuable for those whose home and neighborhood uses of language differ significantly from those which they encounter in school.

Third, conference participants insisted on the need for active learners. They imagined a classroom where students would write for one another as well as for their teachers and where students would listen to and learn from one another as well as from their teachers. They envisioned teachers who would take not only their subject seriously, but also consider who their students are, what they know, and how they can be drawn into their own — and one another's — education. Thus, the tripod became part of a more fully developed scene of dynamic transactions and interactions. In such a view, English teachers are engaged with students in "practicing" — in regularly speaking, reading, writing, and listening to ever-more-varied modes of language; and in learning to reflect, in a self-conscious way, on the powers, beauties, and limitations of these varied uses and usages. Conference participants talked about this second kind of learning as a theoretical activity. When they used the phrase "theorizing about language," they had in mind a self-critical, analytical examination of one's own and others' uses of language. They also had in mind theorizing that assumed control of a body of knowledge: knowledge about language (its grammar, syntax, vocabulary, etc.), about writing (its rhetorical principles and strategies, modes of discourse, etc.), and about literary and other texts (their history, genres, dynamics, and interpretations). Participants assumed that such knowledge would not be gained as a matter of rote learning, but rather would evolve in the course of student "practicing" and involve reflection about what was learned and about those activities that had been pursued in the process of learning.

At all levels of schooling, the group concluded, students need to achieve a broad perspective on their own practices and those that confront them elsewhere in society in order to grapple with the problems of understanding how language works, where the words they hear and their own words come from, and what effects they tend to have. Such critical and self-critical perspectives become accessible to students in classrooms where they know their own words are heard and respected — in classrooms, that is, where teachers' actions demonstrate the precepts they would have students adopt, and where teachers behave consistently with the announced obligation for learners to analyze their own language use. Under these circumstances, students can become sufficiently self-critical to improve their work and adapt what they know to a variety of situations. Similarly, theoretical understanding enables students to recognize when others use language to influence or manipulate them.

Finally, participants concurred on several curriculum issues. They discussed at length the advantages and disadvantages of teaching language arts and English studies in conjunction with lists of various kinds — whether of books, people, events, or concepts. While they agreed that the curriculum at all levels should focus on works that challenge students' abilities as readers and thinkers, they chose not to list what students should read — primarily because prescription often leads to reductive forms of instruction and assessment that defeat the goals of engaging students and fostering judgment as well as the acquisition of facts. The group concluded that just as meaningful education requires content, so does it require active learners.

Aside from recommending children's literature over basal readers, participants advocated that students read widely in both traditional literature and literature that reflects the diversity of American culture, and that they become familiar with as many different kinds of writing as possible (nonfiction as well as fiction, poetry, and drama). Although in practice there is much consensus about what students in our schools should read, the selection of literature for particular courses and classrooms must remain, finally and inescapably, the responsibility of local communities and institutions, guided by the teachers' best judgment and the students' needs and interests.

In the aftermath of the conference, participants were described as supporting "skills" at the expense of "content." As the points of consensus summarized here make clear, however, such a description is far from accurate. The Coalition Conference viewed the skills/ content debate as resting on an overly simple, and ultimately false, dichotomy. Learning inevitably unites skills and content in a dynamic process of practice and assimilation. As Hazard Adams* notes in a recent essay entitled "The Fate of Knowledge," it is precisely this tendency to think of "knowledge as only content or only skill" that has made the debate thus far "seem so arid." As an alternative, Adams suggests that if we "consider knowledge as a process, then it would be possible always to be in it and keep going, and both a past and a future would come into view. It would be a future of questioning and a past consistently queried and reformulated." In many ways, the English Coalition report attempts to put this principle into practice, to envision a curriculum which posits knowledge as process.

From the beginning, the planners felt that it would be impracticable to adopt resolutions verbatim during the 1987 conference itself, but the group agreed to adopt in principle the resolutions that appear in the fourth chapter of this report. These — edited for consistency, brevity, and sufficiency of background detail by Richard Lloyd-Jones

---

*Hazard Adams's essay appears in *Cultural Literacy and the Idea of General Education: The Eighty-seventh Yearbook of the National Society for the Study of Education,* pages 52–68 (Chicago: National Society for the Study of Education, 1988).

and Andrea A. Lunsford — have been reviewed by a committee of members from the different subgroups: Paul Armstrong, Fred Burton, Candy Carter, Carole Edmonds, Phyllis Franklin, Julie Jensen, John Joyce, John Maxwell, George Shea, and Eleanor Q. Tignor.

The English Coalition Conference: Democracy through Language

Report of the Elementary Strand

Today's Elementary School Child

America's elementary school population today resembles a rich, vibrant mosaic — a dynamic composite of children from a variety of cultures, linguistic backgrounds, and religions. Children's ways of knowing and learning reflect changes in society, family, and technology; some of these changes have positively influenced children and their learning, while other changes have been to their detriment.

Changes in Society

Many different kinds of changes in society pose different challenges for today's schools and the children they serve. For example:

- Frequent and extensive geographical redistribution of children and their families, both across country and into urban areas, has caused constantly changing school populations. Variations in student population have brought together students of many races, languages, and religious persuasions.

- Lifestyles emphasizing materialistic values and self-gratification detract from the time for, and the quality of, interaction between children and their families, often resulting in a reduced or inflated sense of self-worth.

Changes such as these can be enriching, exposing students to many different perspectives, but they also can be frustrating for children who have been uprooted from familiar surroundings and who may experience a sense of isolation.

Changes in Family

Changes in family structure and lifestyle affect children from all economic backgrounds. In many family settings, it is difficult to meet the needs of children.

- Families with limited financial resources, who have greater difficulty providing for basic needs such as food, clothing, and shelter,

1

now constitute a larger proportion of the national population. Larger numbers of children are coming to school hungry, malnourished, or tired.

- In increasing numbers of families, the quality and frequency of personal interaction and communication have been reduced. In some instances, there are not enough adults to go around; in others, family members are overscheduled in their activities, with little time left for interacting with one another.

Therefore, children often carry heavy emotional burdens which drain intellectual and creative energy. They may be provided little encouragement or few opportunities for imagining and creating.

Changes in Technology

Children are increasingly influenced by media and technology, which is a mixed blessing.

- Media expose children to a large stock of information and images.
- Technological innovations provide many avenues for manipulating information.
- Media may encourage reading by presenting literary selections in inviting formats.
- Unmonitored listening and viewing may involve large chunks of time and yield undesirable results.

Therefore, children are often sophisticated in their awareness of the world around them and in their abilities to use modern technology. Children who spend large amounts of time watching television and listening to their personal stereos, however, necessarily have little time for other ways of knowing. Such patterns of behavior may change the ways children handle problems: They may see violence, for instance, as a solution and look for "quick fixes" so often enacted in thirty-minute program formats.

These changes create some serious problems for children, but the combination of these factors also gives us children with

- a stronger sense of peer support (without the support of sensitive adults, though, in older children this may degenerate into "peer pressure")
- an extensive store of information
- a more inclusive view of the world than that held by their counterparts fifteen or twenty years ago

The Person We Would Like to See Emerge from the Elementary School Classroom

Our hope is that when children leave the elementary school, they will be well on their way to full participation as citizens. We hope that as individuals, they will be caring and compassionate, respectful and understanding of social and cultural diversity. We want them also to be competent, knowledgeable, and self-confident. Since they will live most of their lives in the twenty-first century, and since we cannot know specifically what they will most need, we want them to leave our classrooms not only with knowledge but also with curiosity, a sense of wonder, and imagination. With those attributes they will maintain an enthusiasm for learning, both in school and in their homes and communities.

Children who have a lifelong love affair with learning emerge from classrooms in which language and language learning have played a central role. Because language is integral to thinking and to human interaction, we believe children should leave elementary school knowing about language — that is, knowing how to read, write, speak, and listen, and knowing why language and literacy are so central to their lives. In more specific terms, the language knowledge, abilities, and attitudes that we would like to see develop in our students include the following:

- That they *be* readers and writers, individuals who find pleasure and satisfaction in reading and writing and who make those activities an important part of their everyday lives, voluntarily engaging in reading and writing for their intrinsic social and personal values.

- That they use language to understand themselves and others and to make sense of their world, and as a means of reflecting on their lives; that they engage in such activities as telling and hearing stories, reading novels and poetry, and keeping journals.

- That they use oral and written language in all its varieties as a tool to get things done, to take charge of their lives, to express their opinions, and to function as productive citizens. Reading, writing, speaking, and listening will, for example, help them succeed in the workplace and conduct other everyday activities like shopping and paying bills. They will, among other things, write letters to editors, read newspapers, fill out forms, and speak persuasively.

- That they leave the classrooms as individuals who know how to read, write, speak, and listen effectively. As competent language users they will:
  - — use prior knowledge to comprehend new oral or written texts
  - — possess a variety of strategies for dealing with unfamiliar words and meanings in texts
  - — respond personally to texts
  - — comprehend the literal messages in texts
  - — read and listen interpretively
  - — read and listen critically
  - — be able to write in a wide variety of forms for a wide variety of purposes and audiences
  - — be able to read varied types of texts, including poems, essays, stories, and expository texts in both print and electronic media
  - — make connections within texts and among texts
  - — use other readers' experiences with, responses to, and interpretations of texts
  - — be able to hear literature, appreciating its sounds and cadences

- That they recognize when language is being used to manipulate, coerce, or control them, and that they use language as an effective response to such attempts.

- That they become language theorists, understanding how they and others around them use oral and written language, and learning how to describe these uses in terms of grammar, syntax, and rhetoric. In writing, they understand how to develop different pieces and what those pieces do. In reading, they notice and monitor their own reading processes and their purposes for reading. Self-evaluation is a key component of their oral and written language activities, one that leads to a sense of ownership of their language.

- That they will have an appreciation and respect for their own language and for the language and culture of others. They will understand enough about the dynamic nature of language, language change, and language variety to be open to and understanding of communications from people of linguistic and cultural groups different from their own. They will have had many opportunities, through reading literature from various cultural groups and interacting orally with a variety of people, to be able and willing to see the world from the perspectives of others. They will not only have a sense of the richness and distinctiveness of the life of particular cultural groups, but also a sense of common humanity.

If the child who arrives in our classroom is to emerge as the person we have just described, the school curriculum must be designed to reflect the best of what we know about child growth and development, about language and language learning, and about good pedagogy. The following section details ways in which we find it useful to think about curriculum.

The Language Arts Curriculum

The Child, the Teacher, and the Curriculum

The curriculum should be flexible enough to embrace the varied background experiences of children and focused enough to assist them in developing a sense of our common humanity, as well as of the diversity of our society.

We believe that the curriculum should not be constrained and fragmented by artificial time blocks of the standardized school schedule or grade-level structure, or by commercial, prepackaged materials chosen without regard to the curricular plans of a particular classroom.

The teacher must have a rich storehouse of developmentally appropriate information and resources in which to interest children and support their learning. Throughout the day, the teacher should observe what the child is interested in and allow for choices within a structured framework.

Conditions for Learning

- Active participation and opportunities to reflect on one's actions
- Personal and interpersonal ways to construct reality through play, talk, writing, reading, imagining, art, dance, movement, music, drama, etc.
- A supportive context in which risk-taking is encouraged
- A context rich in literature and print materials (menus, signs, labels, etc.)
- Observation of role models

Framing the Curriculum

We propose the following alternatives to conventional ways of designing the curriculum.

Alternative One

One way to construct a curriculum (which comes from ideas expressed by Eliot W. Eisner in *The Educational Imagination* [Macmillan, 1979]) requires reconceptualizing the notion of objectives.

• Problem-solving objectives: Unlike performance objectives, the ends are clear, but the means to those ends are open — students use straws to build a three-foot bridge that will hold a pint of milk.

• Expressive objectives: These are objectives in which the means are clear, but the ends are not — the class takes a field trip to the zoo, where many educational possibilities might evolve.

Alternative Two

Another alternative to an objectives-centered curriculum is a policy-centered curriculum. Policies, broad statements based on current theory and research about language learning, are meant to be guidelines for instruction. An example of a policy statement is, "Children will be engaged in writing for various purposes and audiences." Decisions about specific content evolve not only from the opening policy statement but from the shared life of the school community (teachers, students, and administrators) as well as from the local community.

Alternative Three

Thematic planning or webbing provides another viable way for teachers to construct and display curriculum in the classroom in a manner consonant with how children learn language. In a web, teachers and children brainstorm about a topic (e.g., a theme, concept, book) and plan activities that are interdisciplinary. For example, a child who is building and flying paper airplanes may also be mathematically measuring flight distances, drawing up plans, hypothesizing, reading books about flight, and perhaps explaining the concepts behind the activities through oral and written language.

Texts and Tests as Curriculum

The focus and source of all curricular development and assessment must be on the individual learner. Because they are necessarily constructed for mass use, externally developed tests and programs are often of considerably less value to literacy development than those created within the community of teachers and students in particular situations.

Standardized tests constitute only a part of the whole assessment process and are generally more useful for examining programs rather than individuals. Individual assessment must be based on the principles and assumptions about learning theory that support literacy development as described in this document. The ultimate aim of any assessment program (see related resolution on page 41) is to provide a better instructional program for the learner. Because we desire able language learners and users, our assessment strategies and instruments need to focus on literacy development. Our proposed model would consist of a portfolio of the child's work — collected, viewed, and assessed periodically, passed from grade to grade, and used to make instructional decisions and reports to parents. Included in the portfolio would be teacher observations, reading records, writing samples, art samples, varied responses to literature, and other pertinent work samples.

Specifically, basal reading programs provide little opportunity for students to read widely enough because of the overwhelming number of materials to be covered, most of which are based on discrete skills that are unrelated to natural reading processes. In addition, the quality of textbook writing is often poor, the information presented in pieces bearing little relationship to a whole. Such a format makes it very difficult for the child to build schemata or connect ideas. Because the language and content are homogenized, formulaic, and simplified, children do not encounter vocabulary, syntax, or content that adequately prepare them to predict what can be expected within other texts. They are led to believe that reading can yield one static, literal meaning.

A Look inside the Elementary Classroom

The Child and the Teacher

The ideal classroom is a community of learners. As in any community, its members play roles as they spend time with each other. In the effective language arts classroom, teachers are in charge of their teaching and children are in charge of their learning. Important to recognize, however, is the intimate relationship of teacher and learner, each defined in terms of the other.

The teacher is an expert and authority on learning and pedagogy, and in some subject matter fields as well. She is a researcher working both theoretically and practically. She is herself a skillful user of language — a reader and a writer as well as a speaker and listener.

Even before children enter the classroom, she plans, organizes, chooses materials, considers teaching strategies. She sets up a structured learning environment to ensure that the desired academic and social interactions are fostered. These activities become ongoing ones, occurring throughout the school year.

When the teacher works with the children, his role is delicately balanced between that of a manager-director and an enabler-interactor with them and their learning. Interactions involve individuals, small groups, or the whole class. As children read, write, talk, and listen, the teacher accepts and affirms their language. He also helps them extend and expand their language by having them use it — in all modes — to make meaning in all areas of the curriculum. The teacher provides information and direction. More often, he responds thoughtfully to children's efforts — with questions, statements, or even laughter and hugs. The teacher also models appropriate actions and attitudes by sharing his personal interests, his curiosity, his affection and respect for children. He also systematically observes children in informal ways in order to assess their progress toward desired ends.

Children bring to the classroom their language proficiency, their curiosity, their own learning styles, their sense of themselves as learners and as people, and their own special authority and expertise. They develop as active learners by participating in planned activities, thinking and questioning, creating, exploring, experimenting, making choices and decisions, and playing. In the process of acquiring knowledge and skill, children make mistakes, which are valued as part of learning. They become risk-takers as their discoveries and contributions are acknowledged and supported by other members of the classroom community. In an environment of trust and respect, sharing and collaborating between children and among children and adults are the norm.

Sometimes the roles that teacher and children play are shared ones. Both the teacher and children are responsible for being contributing members of the classroom community. Both are evaluators of their progress, sometimes finding reason to celebrate, sometimes finding a need to reconsider and reengage any experience. Both are thinkers. Children think about the experiences they engage in and reflect on their learning. The teacher thinks about the teaching/learning interactions with the children and reflects on how and why. Within the classroom community, both teacher and children are active learners.

The classroom community may also include adults other than the teacher. They may be parents, community volunteers, or specialists within the school, such as librarians, art teachers, or reading specialists.

Other students may also be invited in from time to time. Like the teacher, these helpers can interact with individuals, small groups, or the whole class, depending on the purpose of their involvement. Some may be information sources and role models; others may be listeners, readers, responders, or storytellers; still others may provide various kinds of support and support services, such as funds for special projects or help in typing children's books. Making use of such adults extends the sense of community beyond the walls of the classroom and the school.

The Stuff of the Classroom

The selection of materials used in an effective elementary classroom must be based on the characteristics of the children who will use them. The diversity of the children must be reflected in the variety of materials. The materials must not only reflect the varying learning styles, language proficiencies, and interests of the children, but also be easily and always accessible. Despite the physical and fiscal constraints on room size, wall and floor treatments, and the amount and types of furniture, a classroom can be a learner-centered one in which the organization, variety, and accessibility of materials entice and accommodate the child.

As much as possible, the classroom should extend and bring in experiences from the school, neighborhood, and other overlapping communities to which children belong. Where integration of classrooms or extended classrooms has taken place, children have vast resources of information and interaction.

Classroom Library

Classroom libraries model what we believe about books. The number and diversity of books, the authors we include, the forms of text all represent what we value as texts and what we value as prior knowledge that a child brings to texts. What we exclude we devalue by omission.

Further, classroom libraries model what we believe about becoming lifelong readers. The number and diversity of ways in which children read, respond, get together, and share books — all are conducive to the development of a lifelong reader. The many ways that a classroom library can entice and engage a reader reflect what we believe about the act of reading. A classroom library that celebrates the diversity, backgrounds, interests, and potential of children can include

- a generous ratio of books to students
- books written by children

- books written by community members (other schoolchildren, friends, neighbors, family)
- trade books presenting a variety of genres, areas of interest, and degrees of complexity
- periodicals, magazines, and journals
- print materials such as signs, labels, stickers, box covers, menus, and posters

Writing Materials and Media

A child's world is rich with varieties of writing materials and media: billboards, neon lights, food labels, menus, bumper stickers, tombstones, post-a-notes, birthday cards, and cucumber-shaped pens. The classroom environment can make a very important connection between school and the world outside it by representing at least some of the diversity in writing materials and media that exists outside the school. This diversity can include

- variety in size, shape, texture, and color of "paper" (including poster board and stationery)
- variety of writing implements (including pencils, pens, crayons, novelty pens, felt-tip markers, typewriter, word processor)
- variety of resources (including word lists, thesaurus, spelling checkers, dictionary)
- variety of electronic devices (including tape recorder, record player, computer, video camera, camera, movie camera)

Dramatic Expression and Play

The child's toys become the adult's tools. The roles the child plays become the ways of the adult. Many props can exist in the mind of a child, and there are, in fact, dramatic arts performed without props. But without the space and time for dramatic expression and play, the child cannot rehearse the adult he or she will become. The classroom which values that rehearsal will have

- space for role-playing, dramatization, and improvisation
- a variety of expressive media (including costumes, puppets, masks, and makeup)
- a variety of props (stoves, furniture, store counters, transportation and building models, backgrounds, stage; costumes, masks, makeup; dolls and action figures, puppets; models) a variety of scripts (both

print and nonprint) and activities, such as role-playing, improvisation, comedy, and readers' theater

Artistic Expression

During this developmental period when children are translating concepts and thoughts into symbols, they need opportunities to choose from a variety of graphic as well as alphanumeric translations. Diversity of media increases the possibilities for dialogue among child, picture, and word. Areas in which this dialogue can take place freely

- have a variety of media (including chalk, clay, watercolors, and computer graphics)
- provide opportunities to use artistic expression to complement or supplement language or to act as a catalyst for language
- are easy to clean up

Multisensory Interaction

Children need physical interaction with objects, animals, and plants; they need opportunities to probe and experiment, to hypothesize and test their hypotheses about relationships among the objects of their interaction. At some point, too, children need to be exposed to realistic and abstract representations of their sensory experience and to have an opportunity to compare and contrast these re-creations with their real counterparts. The wider the diversity of real and representational objects, the greater the understanding for the child. Experiences which address all the senses may include

- real objects
- live animals and plants (provide for safety and cleanliness of students, animals, and plants)
- preserved animals and plants
- observation tools (microscopes, thermometers, magnifying glasses, probes)
- realistic and abstract representations for comparing and contrasting with real objects, animals, and plants (artistic and musical representations, photographs, films)
- models (true-to-size models, as well as smaller- and larger-scale models)
- collections

Special Location for Keeping Student Work

A special location where children can keep their work serves many purposes, some as basic as contributing to a sense of organization. For many children, it is important simply to have a place that is wholly theirs. For some, having a central location for drafts and other writings can serve as a record, a way of seeing progress and directions in their language and thoughts. Every student should have a private, individual place to keep his or her work.

Organization

Well-organized time is crucial for developing a stable yet flexible classroom, one that allows for adequate planning and is conducive to learning. Within a five-hour school day, the teacher can weave various aspects of the curriculum into a rich fabric, using large chunks of time to bring naturally related subjects together. When the teacher and children feel free to use time in a fluid and flexible way, they are able to become emotionally, intellectually, and creatively committed to the task at hand, thereby discovering rather than covering the curriculum. They are free to be spontaneous and to savor language and literature.

A flexible attitude toward grouping students allows a community to develop. Rather than establishing several firmly fixed reading groups based on ability and basal readers, for example, the teacher can instead design a literature-based program that invites flexible patterns of grouping children. The whole group, small groups, pairs, or one-to-one meetings are based on children's interests, group dynamics, and personal needs. Interaction among all class members in a variety of settings and for various reasons allows children to invest personally in language learning.

The accessibility and use of materials also contribute to the general tone and organization of a classroom. When children feel free to choose materials, work in a variety of situations, and interact with all class members in an environment that is predictable but not static, exciting but not chaotic, disciplined without being restrictive, they are more likely to become responsible and responsive members of a learning community.

Climate

The climate of the classroom is shaped by the interplay of organization, management, physical environment, and especially by the tone of interactions between teacher and learners. Climate becomes the invisible teacher in the classroom, establishing the foundation for the intellectual, social, and emotional development of the child. We believe that the most effective classrooms convey a sense of order through an environment that is predictable in its schedule and management, as well as in its tone. The security of this environment establishes the foundation for intellectual exploration and risk-taking so necessary for active learning.

The classroom climate must be an honest reflection of the teacher's individual style. Effective climates occur when the teacher has given much thought and preparation to organization and implementation of the structure for the classroom. The teacher knows that there must be limitations and guidelines so that children can engage in real learning experiences, explore options, and make choices in using language to learn.

When teacher and children come together the first day of school, they begin to create a classroom climate. The perceptive teacher listens to children, observes the ways they learn, and finds a variety of strategies to engage children in learning, thus establishing a nurturing climate. Slowly and carefully, teacher and children build a predictable yet fluid structure, within which there is a sense of order as well as freedom of exploration and open interaction. Teacher and children respect and value each other in this climate, as they continually shape a community in which individuals flourish as well as participate as integral members of the group.

Crucial elements that contribute to the climate of the classroom include time, responses, and trust and responsibility.

Time

Children need chunks of time each day to engage in language activities for real purposes. The pace of the classroom is determined partly in response to the development and inquiry of the child. Time is also devoted to play and reflection, because these are valued aspects of learning and growth.

Responses

Teachers need to respond to children in ways which enable the children to explore options, make choices, and participate in meaning-making experiences. Teachers not only bring their expertise and authority to interactions with children, but also nudge and question to stimulate thinking and to enable children to ask their own questions and seek answers.

Trust and Responsibility

Trust assumes that the learner is a human being who has much to give, demonstrate, and teach others. A trusted individual becomes a risk-taker, and to engage in learning is to engage in risk. Trust permits learners to take responsibility for and maintain ownership of their learning.

The goal of the classroom climate is to empower all the learners (children *and* teachers) to seek meaning through reading, writing, listening, and talking and to be continually involved in active inquiry.

Implications for School Administrators, Teacher Educators, and Policymakers

Establishing language arts programs for the twenty-first century in the ways described here will require adaptations by those who create the contexts for education — school administrators, teacher educators, and policymakers who govern the schools. Additional details are suggested in the resolution dealing with "Rights and Responsibilities of Students and Teachers" (see page 45).

School Administrators

- Will be learners who understand children's language growth because they:
  - observe and listen to children in the classroom and throughout the school
  - talk regularly with teachers about their language arts goals and procedures
  - participate with teachers in districtwide inservice programs related to language
  - attend and participate in language-related sessions at meetings of professional associations for administrators
  - read and publish reports of exemplary administrative leadership of language arts programs
- Will support the ongoing learning of teachers and children when they:
  - join with teachers and children in establishing a learning community
  - establish a school professional library which contains materials reflecting current viewpoints about the teaching of language arts, such as those endorsed by professional organizations such as NCTE

— provide time and encouragement for faculty groups to discuss issues and documents of professional concern
— tap the resources of professional associations like NCTE and IRA and their affiliates to enrich inservice education
— encourage teachers to participate in extended educational opportunities beyond the school (e.g., enroll in the National Writing Project, attend conventions of professional associations, participate in summer institutes like those sponsored by the NEH, register for college courses)
— encourage teachers to observe the teaching of their colleagues
— make it possible for teachers to request demonstrations in their classrooms of aspects of language arts teaching
— coordinate efforts to communicate with parents about school language arts goals, instruction, and assessment procedures (e.g., through parent organizations like the PTA, through distribution of materials such as NCTE's "How to Help Your Child Become a Better Writer")
— join with teachers and parents in celebrating learning, rather than grades and test scores; communicate with parents about their child's language growth in clear, informative, and theoretically sound ways
— enlist the aid of the community at large to support the school language arts program (e.g., recruit volunteer aides, develop business contacts, find ways for citizens to serve as resource persons in the classroom, compile a directory of places where teachers may take children to learn outside school)

Educators of Future Teachers

- Will design theoretically sound programs which:
  — view teaching as art, as well as science
  — develop in future teachers a sense of purpose, belief, and commitment to the profession, which will serve as a rationale for their behavior
  — integrate language-related courses, rather than enrolling students in separate courses for reading methods, language arts methods, and children's literature
  — know not only subject matter but children and their ways of language learning (e.g., children's literature professors should know not only books, but the nature of the interactions that may take place between a book and a child)

- — equip future teachers to become "teacher researchers" who continually reflect on the relationship between student learning and their own teaching
- • Will negotiate with elementary school personnel on methods for achieving goals so that
  - — future teachers will receive support from both the college or university supervisor and the cooperating teachers
  - — cooperating teachers will be the finest possible classroom models (possibly on the faculties of "key" or demonstration schools)
  - — college and university administrators and faculty members will work with them in an effort to modify a reward structure which devalues school involvement by faculty
  - — collaborative research between teacher educators and classroom teachers will be encouraged

Policymakers

Policy decisions will be informed by principles of language learning and teaching outlined in this report. Accordingly, legislators, school board members, employees of state and federal agencies, and others will seek the advice of English language arts professionals and their organizations as they:

- • adopt or design instruments for assessing literacy
- • determine the uses of assessment data
- • set priorities for the granting of funds for language-related research
- • make budgetary decisions related to language arts curriculum and teaching (e.g., class size, professional growth opportunities)

Three forces for improving the quality of language arts education for elementary school children are school administrators who are themselves learners and who support the learning of both teachers and children, teacher educators who design theoretically sound programs and who implement them in collaboration with positive classroom models, and policymakers whose decisions rest on sound professional advice.

Report of the Secondary Strand

The secondary strand agreed on the following principles:

1. Learning is the process of actively constructing meaning from experiences, including encounters with a broad range of print and nonprint texts (films, videos, TV and radio advertisements, and so on).

2. Others — parents, teachers, and peers — help learners construct meanings by serving as supportive models, providing frames and materials for inquiry, helping create and modify hypotheses, and confirming the worth of the venture.

3. Learners at different ages and stages of development may well learn in different ways.

The Students*

Increasing numbers of students work during nonschool hours. For some students, such work eliminates participation in extracurricular and cocurricular activities and cuts back on time available for homework. For some, jobs are exhausting and reduce the energy available for schoolwork. For most students, employment distracts attention from school. Although the discipline established on the job can provide valuable lessons, and some jobs offer other useful experience, the fact that large numbers of students in any class hold jobs redefines the school day and challenges the usual priorities of education.

Increasing numbers of students are non-native speakers, and many come from war-torn communities. Although the nation has experienced many waves of immigration, and schools in the past have provided an environment for naturalization, the pressure on schools is growing intolerable as fewer and fewer employment alternatives are available to newcomers. Americans expect universal attendance at school, and society offers few opportunities for unschooled, unskilled labor. In

*See "Illustrations," beginning on p. 51, for portraits of students developed by members of the secondary strand.

addition to language barriers and severe economic problems, many of our refugee students are trying to recover from the traumas of war.

Increasing numbers of students use alcohol and other drugs. The effect of such substances on student health and performance poses a problem in itself, but the underlying social patterns allowing such use are also disruptive. Separation — even estrangement — from parents deprives students of essential emotional support and counsel. Criminal activity, often violent, saps the vitality of academic programs.

Sexual activity is prevalent. Teachers have always had to adapt programs to accommodate the sexual maturation of adolescents, but a mobile and fragmented society has reduced the possibilities for sustained guidance in understanding sexual energies.

Student absenteeism is on the rise. To some extent, this finding grows out of conditions listed above, but whether based on competition from jobs, drugs, or other activities, whether it is permitted by distracted or ineffective parents, or whether it is a response to an ineffective school system and frustration from not finding a place in that system, the effect is to disrupt systematic and sequential approaches to learning. Even when absenteeism is a result of participation in other constructive activities — travel, family vacations, athletic trips, music lessons, and the like — or unavoidable bad ones — illness — individuals lose out on the benefits of participation in a sustained educational program.

Great numbers of students live below the poverty line. Recent studies confirm that poverty is most prevalent among children. Many enrichments normal to educational programs — even basic school materials — often fall beyond the range of family budgets. Moreover, social efforts to improve the nutrition, health, and general welfare of such students are most conveniently and unobtrusively associated with schools and may necessarily divert resources from education to basic sustenance.

Students have increasing difficulty identifying "community standards." As neighborhoods expand to include a rich mix of ethnic and social groups, varying systems of values inevitably present themselves. Students often need help in discovering appropriate ways to evaluate and choose among such varying systems.

Students often respond to fragmented school days and "mass production" education with feelings of isolation and alienation. Active learning requires a sense of community. A teacher who sees 150 or 200 students a day in forty-seven-minute classes for a twelve-week term can neither individualize instruction nor effectively promote students' teaching each other. Such a reality denies what we know about effective learning: that it occurs best in small classes taught by teachers who have time to get to know each student. Even though school districts may be overwhelmed by the costs of providing adequate school buildings near students' homes, sufficient supplies, current educational materials, and competent instruction, students even more need to feel individually important and identifiable within society, and therefore responsible to it.

The Person We Would Like to See Emerge from the Secondary School Classroom

The secondary strand strongly supports the goals articulated by the elementary strand. Secondary teachers especially want all their students to

- use language effectively to create knowledge, meaning, and community in their lives
- reflect on and evaluate their own language use
- recognize and evaluate the ways in which others use language to affect them

The Secondary School Curriculum

The department of English and its classroom teachers are responsible for students' general knowledge of English language and literature, as well as for fluency in reading, writing, speaking, listening, and thinking. Since language is a means by which all other departments teach, these abilities are also called upon in other courses. And since daily living requires constant use of English, learning in the classroom is always affected by activities out of the classroom, few of which are controlled by the teacher. The English curriculum must be flexible enough to adapt to important outside influences and events and to relate to the ways language is used throughout the curriculum. At the same time, it must help build a sense of community among students, teachers, and their common texts. Useful guidelines can be offered in each of five areas.

Language

Students need to learn how to use dictionaries, thesauruses, and guides to usage, as well as how to make systematic observations of how they and others use language. This ability requires at least some introduction to theories of language and to systems for describing language. Since native speakers have learned how to use the basic forms of their language long before puberty, the emphasis should fall on understanding the bases of choice among language forms, rather than on rote exercises. Problems of usage, for example, are best treated in terms of the social implications of particular choices rather than as forms that are correct or incorrect. The history of English is important not only because it indicates both how language changes and how it reflects the community which uses it, but because issues of social identification and adaptation arise naturally in the study of older literature and sophisticated dictionaries. The abstract study of grammar, syntax, semantics, and discourse theory can be valuable as part of the study of the nature of language, and can foster ability to read complex texts. The most effective way to relate such abstractions to the written performance of students, however, is to practice systematic analysis and description of *the students' own writing.*

Reading/Literature

Because reading is a basic part of all academic study, improving reading ability becomes a goal for every academic class. The program in English, however, systematically examines many kinds of writing in order to improve students' general skills in interpretation. Literature provides many of the texts for study, but students also need to work with many other kinds of writing to become attuned and accustomed to different kinds of reading. Student writing itself is important as material for close analysis, with television, advertising, video, specialty magazines, film, and technical reports also providing appropriate texts for study.

Literary study offers students insights into human values expressed in times and places far removed from their own and helps them interpret experiences within their immediate worlds. They should be invited to read deeply in our diverse literary traditions, including writing by men and women of many racial, ethnic, and cultural groups. Literature makes real the cultures we inherit, as well as those of people different from us; it raises fundamental questions of value. Because literature by its very nature presents various views of reality and truth, some people or groups will inevitably try to mandate reading lists to "fit" some particular political or social agenda. The obligation of the English teacher is to represent a range of readings sufficient to exhibit multiple human possibilities and to demonstrate a broad sweep of American cultures as they are embodied in literary texts. Balancing the total reading list in relation to students' needs and experiences requires professional judgment about particular classes and even about particular students, so ample library resources are essential, as is time for teachers to supervise individual reading. As a rule, texts should be presented in their complete form.

Writing

Writing is important as a means for communicating knowledge and opinions to others, and as a means for exploring ideas and feelings and making them precise. For some teachers in some fields, writing is simply the evidence that a student has done work leading to a conclusion; in English, however, the teacher must be concerned with how students arrive at those conclusions as well as with how they finally present their arguments. Students need help in identifying problems or topics to be written about; in discovering principles to organize their ideas, notes, and drafts; in mastering techniques for discovering and testing additional information to develop ideas; in choosing appropriate language for representing their ideas; and in preparing manuscripts.

Such goals are best served by group activities, where students are readers and consulting editors as well as writers, and where teachers act as facilitators and coaches. Classroom discussion of writing in progress helps students understand the reactions of audiences, and classroom publication encourages respect for conventional manuscript form. The act of writing itself helps writers discover relationships among pieces of information acquired from disparate sources. How one thinks is inevitably exposed in writing, so fellow students and teachers (through discussion) can validate a student's ability to formulate ideas.

Since "correctness" and manuscript neatness are important social considerations in writing, the curriculum must deal with such issues, but they must not dilute the concentration on writing as a means to learn. For most students, the opportunity to present their writing to audiences beyond the teacher is sufficient to ensure a concern for the manuscript (information about formats can be presented incidentally to augment what was taught in elementary school). For some students, however, various kinds of learning difficulties or social experiences create special barriers to writing conventionally in edited American English. For students who exhibit these problems, rote exercises serve little purpose; standard exercises are also frequently counterproductive and time-wasting. Special programs — such as those developed to aid dyslexic students, for example — should be widely available.

Speaking/Listening

These activities are often taken for granted and neglected, perhaps because they seem pervasive. Yet students need systematic help in assimilating the discussion that takes place in class and in conducting disciplined discussion in pairs, small groups, or whole classes. Because learning most often takes place in some form of interaction, usually involving other people, instruction on how to work efficiently in small committees is important. Systematic listening in discussions or to lectures also requires practical skill. Much of this work can be developed naturally in conjunction with reading and writing assignments, but progress requires more than classroom interrogation or recitation. Oral reading, dramatic performances, and similar activities of both classroom writing and assigned literature can also be useful in helping students edit their own writing and interpret texts more sensitively.

Thinking

Although "higher-order thinking skills" have become part of catchword solutions to problems of education, thinking is hard to describe separately from specific learning in all of the subjects of a school. Most thinking processes are also a means of using language, though, so writing and reading with a concern for whole works (in contrast to excerpts) are natural activities for exhibiting patterns of thought. In contrast, some modern testing programs may isolate information and encourage passive ingestion of "facts," especially in large lecture formats, but classrooms that encourage presentation of lines of thought and reasoning and that offer opportunities for persuasion will teach thinking. Some concern for formal logic, statistical generalizations, or other forms of thinking is appropriate, but highly formalistic approaches to thought should not be ends in themselves.

The Classroom and Teaching Styles

The classroom environment often dominated the discussion of teaching in the secondary strand. The group concluded that because language is inherently social, classroom procedures should be interactive, supportive, orderly, individualized, and varied. The teacher is primarily a coach, a skilled practitioner of the arts the students need to acquire. At times a coach simply offers information as in a lecture, but usually a coach sets tasks, comments on performances, encourages the weary and fainthearted, identifies sources of information, and finally holds the course toward general goals, giving order to many variations.

Interactions

Language is mastered by practice, so an English classroom encourages purposeful talk and listening, as well as periods of silence for individual writing and reading. A teacher coaches students on writing in progress or on interpreting literature and plans activities so that students understand not only what is expected, but why it is expected. Students thus learn to adapt the techniques they discover to other occasions. Interaction implies a commitment of time, to making the class into a community of learners who recognize their obligations as collaborators with their companions and as negotiators for common goals.

Support

Making statements in writing or speech involves risks of failure, often in quite public ways. Some students, in reaction to their own problems, undermine the confidence of others, so teachers must be especially alert to encourage the diffident. Even resisting temptations merely to "follow the crowd" may require help from the teacher. Because language is personal as well as social, teachers of English must devote time and energy to appreciating individual variations in student performances.

Order

Communities are orderly by definition, as language is. They cannot exist without a sense of what people expect of one another. Classroom communities are often disrupted by outside activities, by misbehavior, and by ordinary absence. If the group is large and comes together for short periods in short academic terms, it often cannot develop its own sense of order, and externally imposed order is a poor substitute. Reading most literature requires sustained effort over large blocks of time, in school or out. After rumination and discussion, productive writing requires sustained and uninterrupted time. Discussion itself takes time to develop. The amount of intervention by the teacher should be less and less obvious as students mature and develop their capacities for self-regulation, but even a group of mature adults ordinarily identifies leadership in managing its affairs. Teachers must be prepared to nudge discussions into useful questioning. The challenge is to support orderliness in ways that allow each student to achieve the most individual growth.

Individuality

Students rarely, if ever, fit into neatly defined categories. Their wide variety of backgrounds and experiences ensures an equally varied response to texts. Because reading and writing depend so significantly not only on texts but on individual performance, ideal instruction must allow for individual variations. Thus, while particular literary texts and particular writing experiences should perhaps be offered to all our students, the time of offering and manner of presentation must allow for variations in student needs.

Classroom Format

The broad range of information, activities, and skills characteristic of English classes calls for flexibility in classroom scheduling. Reading and writing often demand sustained periods of peace and quiet; while arriving at consensus, deriving interpretations, and revising texts require carefully sequenced discussions and other activities. The traditional school period and day seldom allow for such flexibility and variation.

In order to achieve the goals described in this report, our secondary schools must move quickly to

- reduce fragmentation and interruptions of the "normal" secondary school day by providing for more sustained work periods
- allow for more sustained relationships between teachers and students
- involve teachers actively in academic decision making
- define normal teacher load as four classes of twenty students
- improve libraries and other resources, such as computer facilities and data bases

Report of the College Strand

College Students Today

Changes in the student population affect college classroom practices just as they do elementary and secondary practices. In general, college students are older than they used to be; more culturally and linguistically diverse; more immersed in the appeals of television and other media, including advertising; and more likely to hold jobs, to attend college part-time, and to take longer to complete their studies. Much of the first two years of undergraduate teaching occurs in two-year colleges, which often necessarily stress immediate vocational or occupational goals. In short, our students often have dramatically different backgrounds, goals, and work experiences from those of previous college generations.

The Person We Would Like to See Emerge
from the College Classroom

The college strand strongly endorses the elementary strand's description of the persons we would like to see emerge from our classrooms: Students, whatever their age, who are active learners and who are able to reflect critically on their own learning. We want to enable students to use and understand language in general and English in particular, as they practice speaking, writing, listening, and reading in ways appropriate to different purposes and in varying circumstances. Our aim is to develop students with a high degree of practical and theoretical literacy, whose command of language is exemplary. Such a goal rests on the assumptions that the arts of language (reading, writing, speaking, and listening) are social and interactive and that meaning is negotiated and constructed. We believe that students should learn to write, read, and reflect on texts from multiple perspectives.

The College Curriculum

We recommend that English studies be based on *practices* — the activities of engaged reading, writing, speaking, and listening, followed

25

by extensive reflection on those practices. Literary, learning, and rhetorical theories, as well as the connections among them, support the changes we advocate throughout English studies, from freshman writing through advanced work. The structuring of the English curriculum around writing and reading as complex processes does not necessarily require abandoning either the canon of traditional literature or courses organized around author, period, or genre. But it does call for including a wide range of previously excluded works, including those by women and racial and ethnic minorities and those that come to us through media other than printed texts. As indicated here, we also believe it is important to teach traditional works in relation to theoretical concerns. Central to the proposals that follow is the principle that writing, reading, speaking, and listening should be integrated in the English curriculum. True integration means, among other things, that the acts of speech and writing, not only in response to texts that are read but as a means of exploring and communicating one's own ideas and experience, deserve as prominent a place in the English curriculum as the acts of reading and responding to texts written by others. Because English departments have historically privileged reading over writing, we must strike a new balance by emphasizing the importance of writing in both our curricula and our research programs.

While we address teacher education explicitly only in the additional resolutions (see next chapter), all the proposals that follow have strong implications for the training of teachers. Our emphasis on practices has clear connections with pedagogy, and thus we recommend collaboration with faculty in education and with precollege teachers and administrators in designing effective teacher education programs. The growth of composition and rhetoric as a subfield of English has already moved us to attend to the pedagogical matters, as have recent developments in literary theory (e.g., the interest of reader-response theorists in students' response to literature). As we focus our attention on how people read and write, we naturally become concerned with how they *learn* to read and write.

Freshman Writing and Reading

Rationale

The effective uses of language, which are at the heart of English studies, are of increasing importance to a democratic society. Future citizens will be required to manage enormous amounts of information, in language directed to various audiences and designed to fulfill particular purposes. In an information age, citizens need to make meaning — rather than merely consume information — in informal, formal, imaginative, and analytic ways and in many settings. English teachers need to provide the kinds of writing and other language experiences — reading, speaking, listening — that will enable students, both alone and collaboratively, to develop strategies for interpreting and organizing information. At the same time, these experiences must be diverse enough to prepare citizens for the demands of a pluralistic society. Such experiences will also enable students to use language to make sense of their lives.

The work of many cognitive developmental psychologists and ethnographic researchers (see Appendix D) stresses the relationship between active participation and learning. Others in psychology, anthropology, and learning theory argue for the strong relationship between collaboration and effective learning, a relationship explored in much current composition and literary theory.

We therefore propose designing a yearlong, entry-level course that will use current theory and research to focus on the uses of language; the value-laden nature of all such uses; and the ways we and our students use writing, reading, speaking, listening, and critical thinking to construct ourselves as individuals and as members of academic and other communities. Such a course would stress an *active, interactive theory of learning* (rather than a theory of teaching), one that assumes students do not learn by being passive eavesdroppers on an academic conversation or vessels into which knowledge is poured. This course would integrate reading, writing, speaking, and listening and would build on what students already know. It would offer a basis for their continued language development as individuals, immediately in the academy and later in other communities.

Principles of Organization

One possible version of such a course sequence might focus on how language shapes and is shaped by the self, by communities, and by society. As students investigate the construct of self, they might read autobiographical texts, write journal entries or narratives designed to render their own experiences, collect and analyze samples of their own idiolects, and present the findings of these investigations in formal and informal class presentations. As the focus shifts to the construct of communities, students might collaborate to study the language structures of a particular workplace, an extended family or other social group, or an academic discipline. Students might write extended field notes based on observations of particular language communities, read and discuss texts that describe such communities, and work together to compile and annotate lexicons for specialized communities. Such activities might lead to a formal analytical essay or oral presentation. As students explore how the United States manifests its national identity in various linguistic constructs, they might examine the language of print and electronic media, politics, religion, law, or medicine. Increasingly, students will develop their own theories from their observations and analyses, and reflect on and evaluate the implications of their theories.

Such a sequence would require redesigning the freshman English course around three basic principles: investigation or critical inquiry, collaboration, and conscious theorizing. The principle of critical inquiry suggests that students are in active control of their learning — using, analyzing, and evaluating language within different contexts. The collaborative model suggests that the teacher acts as an informed and challenging coach, offering multiple perspectives, while students practice and experience the kind of cooperation all citizens increasingly need. The concept of conscious theorizing about their learning and about how language works (and to what ends it works in various contexts) allows students to understand the principles they follow and so enables them to transfer what they learn.

Practical Implications

The learning theories which inform this description of freshman English have several implications. To make possible the interaction and writing central to active learning, classes need to be limited to twenty students and scheduled to allow time for students to engage actively and interactively in the process of learning (fifty-minute classes and nine-week quarters all too often undermine inductive learning). Developmental courses need to be informed by the same theories of learning, which integrate writing, reading, speaking, and listening, rather than focus on discrete subskills. These developmental classes, however, need to be somewhat smaller (no more than fifteen students) to allow for even more individual and interactive experiences.

Another significant implication relates to the preparation of those who teach this new, yearlong course. All such teachers must be educated in pertinent aspects of learning theory, current literary and reading theories, and current writing theory and practice. Major changes in student populations also suggest that teachers of the freshman sequence will increasingly need a thorough grounding in language structures, particularly as those structures relate to American dialects, English as a second language, and English as a foreign language. In institutions where teaching assistants or other adjunct faculty teach the new courses, these teachers must be guaranteed preparation in theory and practice. Teachers will also need professional growth opportunities, including networking and collegiality, teacher-as-learner experiences, application of learning at the home institution, administrative involvement, and connections between new information and the best of the old (the emphasis on collaboration, discovery, process, and teacher-as-coach associated with both writing-across-the-curriculum and writing-process movements).

General Education in the Humanities

General education is, in a sense, the most amorphous part of the humanities curriculum. Its goals are perhaps less easily definable and more ambitious than the aims of a major. But the purposes that general-education courses in the humanities should serve for our students are extraordinarily important. In the English courses designed for general education, students should learn to participate intelligently and ethically in the discourses of the communities to which they do and will belong as citizens.

Rationale

A deep, rigorous coherence in undergraduate humanities education can best be achieved by creating courses that explore key conceptual questions. Such courses should center on problems which introduce students to different ways of reading, writing, and thinking. These courses should include a variety of texts from within the traditional canon as well as from alternatives to it. The problems and the ways of reading and writing around which this kind of course is organized need not, and indeed cannot, try to "cover" the humanities, but they should engage students in ways of thinking and interpreting which will be useful to them in other humanistic contexts.

Although introducing students to the implications of multiple ways of making meaning is the main mission of these courses, knowing how to understand cannot be taught apart from some issue or text which the course is trying to come to terms with. These courses should be organized around problems through which "knowing about" becomes an occasion to raise questions about "knowing how" and "knowing why." There are no preset limits which define what these problems can or should be. Indeed, a course on well-established, classical works could be conceptualized in a manner which would focus attention on different ways of reading and on cultural diversity — especially if, for example, such a course asked how these texts might be read by a Hispanic or black student (regardless of gender), a woman (regardless of color), or a member of a third-world culture; or if works traditionally excluded from formal study were included so that the process of canonization could be examined. Such a course would treat traditional canonical texts not as sacred icons to be merely revered, but as human, historical creations that are preserved as long as they serve a changing array of cultural purposes.

Developing an awareness of language should be a major goal of these courses. An important reason for epistemological and cultural heterogeneity is that knowledge is language-bound and that language is extremely malleable. One of the best ways to learn about language and reading is to write, and writing should be an integral part of general-education humanities courses. This goal demands that students write frequently. Assignments should encourage students to use writing as a means of discovery — a way to experiment with the ideas of the course, to explore their implications, and to find out what they themselves think. Such assignments would be a productive continuation of a restructured freshman English course which integrated writing and reading. The aim in both parts of the curriculum would be to help students learn how to write, read, listen, speak, and think through interactive instruction. At all levels of education, students should experience the value of writing as a tool of inquiry and become increasingly confident of their ability to express themselves clearly and to think critically. They should learn to write in order to conceptualize and to conceptualize in order to write.

General-education programs should also take advantage of regional variations and institutional differences. Given the variety of interests, needs, and resources of different institutions, teachers, and students across the country, the problems these courses focus on and the texts they include should and will vary widely. Organizing general education around key problems which dramatize differences between ways of reading and which explore cultural diversity offers a curricular scheme that encourages individual variation. This approach to general education will allow flexibility in the curriculum without sacrificing coherence. Although these courses may be extremely diverse in content and theme, they share a conceptual focus — their concentration on multiple ways of reading, writing, and thinking — and a common view of how we use these communicative arts to create, examine, and choose among systems of value.

Principles of Organization

In an age of interdisciplinary study and blurred boundaries between regions of knowledge, it is difficult to demarcate a clear, precise boundary between the role English departments should play in general education and the contributions other humanities departments should make. General education is necessarily a cooperative venture, and each humanities discipline will bring different perspectives to it. The organizing principle governing all general education in the humanities, however, should be to introduce students to the implications of multiple ways of reading, writing, and thinking about the problems of any culture, including our own.

Lists of any kind risk becoming prescriptive, thus limiting the imagination and creativity of teachers who should be encouraged to tailor general-education courses to their knowledge and interests and to the interests and needs of their students. Without exemplars that suggest concretely what such a course might look like, however, a proposal for curricular change can lack the force and clarity it should have. The following examples of possible general-education courses in the humanities are consequently offered as illustrations, without any sense that this list is inclusive or definitive.

- Knowledge and language in the sciences and the humanities
- Interpretation and texts in Eastern and Western cultures
- Metaphor in language and cognition
- Change in literary and nonliterary history
- Reading in print and other media
- Dialects and the relativity of "Standard English"
- "Great Books" and the process of canonization
- Racial and sexual difference in reading and writing
- The concept of "genre" in writing and interpretation

Practical Implications

Many of these courses will be interdisciplinary in approach and theme. When faculty members from different departments decide to team up to teach a course on a problem of mutual interest, their institution should give them as much concrete support as it can. Team-teaching across disciplinary boundaries is a challenging enterprise which often requires more time than ordinary courses do.

Courses in general education need to be designed with their own special aims in view and *should not* simply be taken from existing courses in the English major. The way these courses are taught should be compatible with their themes and aims. The primary mode of instruction should be discussion in which students learn, through their own experience in the classroom, that different ways of thinking and reading are possible. Teaching by discussion requires small classes. Discussion is generally preferable to lecture, because students learn most effectively when they are actively involved in the process of discovery. But in courses aimed at helping students develop an awareness of the diversity of their culture and an ability to analyze and react to it intelligently, it is especially important that the different points of view that arise in discussion be a central focus of the course itself. Allowing for such discussion will demand relatively small classes.

The English Major

Background

Over the past twenty years there have been major reevaluations of issues central to the discipline of English, such as the place of writing in the curriculum, the status of the reader, the nature of textuality, the social construction of language, the relationship between theory and practice, gendered reading and writing, and canon formation. We have seen the development of the new historicism and the addition to the canon of works by authors previously excluded because of gender, race, ethnicity, and class. Videos and other forms of popular culture have become appropriate areas of study, indicative of a shift from literary to literary and cultural studies.

The ADE ad hoc committee on the English major, in its recent nationwide study of English departments, discovered considerable change since Thomas Wilcox's study of some twenty years ago (published as *The Anatomy of College English*). Most notable has been the addition of majors in various kinds of writing and, with them, the hiring of faculty members trained in composition and rhetoric. Less change appears in literature majors: courses are predominantly organized by period, genre, and major authors; they primarily concern themselves with canonical literary texts (poetry, fiction, drama); and their goals are formal and/or historical analysis. Nevertheless, the

ADE study suggests that, in general, while the same texts are taught that were taught thirty years ago, they are increasingly taught in ways informed by new questions. Curricula and departments are changing and will continue to change in an evolutionary, accretive manner. We urge an increase in the rate of change, with respect to curricula but also to faculty and the organization of departments: As we advocate according greater importance to the role of writing in curricula, so we advocate equity for those who teach it.

All students majoring in English should read a wide variety of texts and engage in diverse types of writing. They should be able to inquire into the complex functions of language, especially in relation to their own and other cultures; the ways in which meanings are created; the nature of literature; the relationships between readers and texts, authors and texts, literature and society, and reading and writing in their experiential and historical dimensions. Such an English major will enhance students' ability to think critically about these problems, none of which is esoteric or purely theoretical. The increased ability to read, write, and, above all, to reflect critically will help students analyze and understand the complex ideological forces that help to shape the diversity of texts they encounter daily.

Rationale

Over ten years ago, Jonathan Culler* called for teachers of English to mitigate their near obsession with interpretation, a concern that, he argued, is "only tangentially related to the understanding of literature," and to focus on the "conventions and operations of an institution, a mode of discourse." Other such proposals have been heard over the past few years, as the issues that have altered the thinking of the profession have begun to be translated into curricular and pedagogical practice. Robert Scholes wants the object of our study to be textuality. Arac, Messenger, and Sorensen argue for hermeneutics, poetics, and criticism. McCormick, Waller, and Flower suggest language, history, culture, and a focus on the cognitive and cultural aspects of reading and writing. Nelson emphasizes textuality and culture.

While there are differences among these positions, what each has in common is the recognition that as students learn to reflect on their own practices in reading and writing, they will become more self-aware, more independent and strong as readers and writers. It is significant that a number of these positions have already been translated

---

*Jonathan Culler's essay, "Beyond Interpretation: The Prospects of Contemporary Criticism," appeared in 1976 in *Comparative Literature* 28:244–65.

into curricula: In *Professing Literature,* Gerald Graff lists more than a dozen departments that have moved in the directions we propose, specifically from programs in literary studies to programs in literary and cultural studies.

The issue of history (or more accurately, histories) is especially important. In the past, while literary history has often driven the curriculum of English studies, the idea of history — and how we make sense of the past — has been missing; rather, it has been assumed that coverage of a chronological span will add up to a sense of history. Coverage alone is an undesirable goal if it takes the place of serious inquiry into the problem of history. Coverage is also an increasingly unrealistic expectation: While complete coverage of a period in a course has never been fully possible, the recent expansion of the canon makes the notion of coverage even more problematic.

What students have to infer from period courses should become part of the curriculum. The alternative proposed here is to make literary history itself an object of study by investigating the nature of historical inquiries, historical transitions, and periodization, so that students can begin to recognize how they themselves are involved in them. For example, a course might begin by looking at some competing or overlapping descriptions of the shift from Renaissance to Classical ways of thinking and writing. T. S. Eliot's term for this shift — "dissociation of sensibility" — could provide a point of departure. The first hundred pages of Michael Foucault's *The Order of Things* could be used to challenge and complicate Eliot's scheme by introducing a description of the Renaissance and Classical "epistemes" or ways of making sense of the world. These could be tested by contrasting texts of such Renaissance writers as Hooker, Donne, and Sidney with those of such neoclassical writers as Pope, Hume, and Fielding. Depending on circumstances, texts in other media such as architecture, painting, sculpture, and music might also be included, along with the periodizing terminology of art historians, music historians, and social, political, and economic historians. The point of such a course would not be to apply Eliot or Foucault, but rather to test their theories and refine or even refute them.

Principles of Organization

Intellectual developments and social change challenge accustomed ways of situating the discipline in a curricular structure. Nonetheless, unified by a conviction that the major should take advantage of both the polemical energies change has brought to the field and the rich literature available for study, the college strand reached a consensus about a general itinerary for all English majors. This would provide a set of common experiences within a department's specialized degree programs, whether in writing, literature, media studies, or cultural studies.

1. All English majors should know several methodologies of reading and interpretation, be acquainted with the premises and the modes of arguing that each pursues, and be aware of issues connected with a choice of one perspective versus another. Examples of such methods of reading and interpretation include aesthetic, biographical, formalist, gender-specific, rhetorical, and political.

2. All English majors should know something of the critical and historical principles behind the construction of literary and cultural histories. They should know the terminology of literary periods, be aware of controversies concerning the establishment of distinctions between periods, and understand the general significances attached to various views taken of the transitions between periods. They should also have opportunities to examine the status of the concept of nationality as it appears in literary study.

3. All English majors should know something about the study of language and discursive practices. Avenues to such knowledge include study in the history of the language, formal grammar and rhetoric, psycholinguistics and sociolinguistics, and semiotics.

4. All English majors should have the experience of reading texts drawn from the full diversity of literary periods and genres, written by authors representing the full range of social, ethnic, and national origins that have contributed to the corpus of literature in English. They should also have experience with critical texts and with expository prose and other types of writings that have frequently not been made use of in the curriculum of the major, including writing by their fellow students.

5. All English majors should practice writing in several modes and for different audiences and purposes, with an awareness of the social implications and theoretical issues these shifts raise. Classroom practice should bring teachers and students to experience writing, reading, listening, and speaking as integrated, mutually supporting exercises.

Practical Implications

What classroom practices follow from this restructuring of the major? If we teach from an intentional theoretical position and expect students to make connections among the courses they elect, we change the classroom from a place in which knowledge is disseminated to one in which — as students examine and criticize the production of knowledge — learning occurs and knowledge is created. The changes we propose for the major are all the more important given the Holmes Report's recommendations on teacher training.* Recent developments in literary and rhetorical theory encourage our having students focus on issues relevant to teaching — issues such as how we understand texts; how readers make meaning; how readers, authors, and texts interact. An issue-centered curriculum is a learning-centered curriculum, one that is, moreover, compatible with a student-centered curriculum.

It follows, therefore, that courses in English education should emphasize learning rather than teaching, and that they be accompanied by courses in learning theory and adolescent development. The English major we propose, with its emphasis on how to do English rather than what English is, will better address the needs of preservice and inservice teachers. The models that college English instructors will offer teachers preparing to work at all levels (elementary, secondary, and tertiary) will place a self-conscious emphasis on the major issues in English studies. Teachers can thus see that addressing questions of sending and receiving messages in texts of all kinds will aid their students in realizing the power of language. The questions that teachers ask, in accord with this model, will become the following: "How do people learn from texts?" "How does one read a text?" "How does the teaching of texts in particular ways affect the ways students learn about them?" "How does the classroom construct knowledge?"

---

*Published in 1986, the recommendations appear in *Tomorrow's Teachers: A Report of the Holmes Group* (East Lansing, Michigan).

Additional Resolutions

The following additional resolutions were prepared by various coalition subgroups and approved in general terms by the whole conference.

The Place of Media Studies in English/Language Arts

The media have no doubt had both good and bad effects on the students who come to our classrooms at all levels. Nonetheless, our entire culture has changed because of the presence of electronic media in our homes. The media provide many of the major texts by which the world is presented to students and by which students perceive the world.

Students need to know a wide range of strategies for approaching symbol systems and to learn methods of analyzing the logic and argument of these systems. Electronic technologies supplement and alter literacy as it has been traditionally defined. Affirming our responsibility for reading and writing in print, we must meet the challenge of teaching print literacy in an electronic culture. Schema theory and psychology now tell us that intelligence is not simply linear, any more than learning is merely linear and accretive. Images form the basis of abstraction and generalization in ways equally powerful to those of traditional logic and argument.

The electronic curriculum includes study about the forms of culture developing within the new technologies, as well as the practices of writing in the new technologies. We call for research to develop new educational uses of these technologies. In addition, we call for cooperation across fields of knowledge for studying the effects and applications of electronic media in society.

As English language arts teachers develop the curriculum for students, they must also realize the possibilities for professional growth and management now offered by the field of telecommunications. Electronic mail and bulletin boards, with their capability to manage, exchange, and store information, offer sources for teachers to make connections and grow through collegiality.

The mere presence of the technology, of the machines in themselves, will not bring about the kind of study and growth here described. Nonetheless, the machines provide tools for communication and interaction. They have freed us from the mechanics of mere storage and transmission of knowledge and offered creative possibilities for new ways of seeing and doing, when used by sensitive and trained teachers.

Finally, we call for research which will tell us more directly than we presently know whether the electronic media are restructuring the ways people process information. We need research on the effects of electronic media on cognition. We need to understand more clearly than we now do how electronic media, viewing behavior, reading, and literacy are related.

English as a Foreign Language

Many college English departments expect that students have mastered the fundamentals of English prior to admission, viewing their students as relatively homogeneous in using spoken English. Such assumed homogeneity is misleading. In fact, many college students are from other countries where English is not the primary language; many more are Americans for whom English is a second language, acquired after mastery of their first language (for example, residents of Puerto Rico, Hispanic students, refugees from various wars around the world, recent immigrants and their children). This already large population is increasing at a rate which, if continued, will become close to a majority of American students by the year 2000.

These students require an emphasis on language skills at all levels of instruction, in spite of the fact that such an expansion is not characteristic of the traditional literature-based curriculum or even of grammar studies. For such individuals, advanced study in the language is difficult or impossible until the fundamental, tool-using skills of English are mastered. The skills may range from simple spoken communication to the relatively complex skills of reading and writing. In the absence of such language fluency, effective communication is prevented by the inherent barrier posed by any non-native language. In spite of such communication difficulties, however, most non-English-fluent students are academically capable and should not be identified with those who require remedial instruction.

A variety of instructional programs has been developed for such students, including English as a Foreign or Second Language (ESL/

EFL),* bilingual education, special tutorial or content sections of particular courses, and English for Specific Purposes (ESP). A common characteristic of these programs is a focus on the *use* of English and the use of instructional strategies more characteristic of foreign language classes, such as French or Spanish, than of the structural and literary content studied in English as a Native Language (ENL) classes.

Where programs for preparing teachers exist, they tend to conform to the guidelines of the Teachers of English to Speakers of Other Languages (TESOL) and are concerned with the preparation of teachers for state certification or the master's degree in the teaching of EFL/ESL. In only a few instances, however, can such programs be found in departments of English; favored loci tend to be special adjunct programs not usually within the academic "general-education" province.

A major consequence of such programs, whether for teacher education or student preparation, is that neither their teachers nor their students are considered to be part of the "traditional academic track," and the instruction provided is not seen as contributing to the institutional program. When one group has little or no contact with the standard content of the English curriculum, both groups necessarily suffer later when they are integrated in other subject areas. Another consequence is that students in such ESL/EFL programs usually require longer periods of study time to achieve the desired diploma or degree than do other students, leading to invidious structuring, in which some students discover that their instructional costs are much higher than those of their peers.

For all the reasons adduced here, and because ESL/EFL students will constitute approximately forty percent of the student population by 2000, we call for the following changes within English programs at all levels:

- Increased emphasis on language study within all areas of the English curriculum

- Recognition that most ESL/EFL courses represent language courses rather than remedial or supplementary courses

---

*ESL is usually viewed as English for students whose home language is other than English and who will be resident in the United States for most of their lives; EFL is English language instruction for international students who will require English proficiency as a fact of academic study and professional use, but who will normally be resident in their non-English-speaking home countries. In common practice, ESL usually refers to elementary- and secondary-level instruction, with EFL the college-level equivalent, although such designations are frequently interchanged.

- Recognition of ESL/EFL as a scholarly academic area whose practitioners are recognized as coequals with their English department colleagues
- Greater attention to the responsibilities of college-level English departments for teacher education directed toward both ENL and ESL/EFL students
- Increased communication within and across college departments among the member organizations of the English Coalition and other language organizations, including TESOL, IATESOL, ADFL, and ACTFL
- Greater responsibility for English departments and for related professional organizations (MLA, NCTE, CCCC) to lead the way in addressing concerns of ESL/EFL and in planning for the future; such leadership might result in joint conferences, institutes, or other formal means of intercommunication

Tracking at Elementary and Secondary Levels

Tracking and ability-grouping are perpetuated by the assumption that teachers can better meet individual needs in groups of homogeneously grouped students. In *A Place Called School* (McGraw-Hill, 1984), John Goodlad calls this assumption "a retreat rather than a strategy" (297) — in particular noting the differences in teaching modes that emphasize rote learning and skills practice in low tracks, but "higher-order" thinking skills in high tracks, a dichotomy that denies "low-track" students the "types of instruction most highly associated with achievement" (155).

In addition, tracking systems in many schools have the effect of segregating learners along lines that are primarily racial or ethnic. In this way, and because such segregation prevents a richness of experience for high- and low-track students which mixed classes provide, the hidden curriculum demonstrated by tracking promotes elitism of certain learning styles, modes of expression, and cultural and ethnic views.

When learners are separated by ability or skill level into reading groups or ability-grouped classes, they suffer from the lack of interaction with learners of different abilities. We recommend, therefore, that students studying the same subject *not* be assigned to classes on the basis of past performance or testing, and that teachers be trained to modify classroom practices in order to offer equitable educational opportunities within heterogeneous groupings in all classrooms.

Statement on Testing and Assessment

During the past ten to fifteen years, the amount of assessment — especially large-scale assessment — has increased at all levels of education. Assessment can present a problem: It often reflects a breakdown of trust in schools and teachers; it sometimes has the effect of discouraging students from going to college; and at all levels it heightens a competitive mentality in school and often harms students' attitudes toward schooling and toward themselves.

In recent years, the increased call for assessment of student learning has often resulted in a curriculum that is test- and assessment-driven. That is, what students learn and how they learn it is now, at least in part, determined by the various assessments that have been imposed on elementary and secondary schools and sometimes on colleges. Often those directly concerned with the education of students have little or no say in determining what will be tested, how, why, when, or under what circumstances. For example, many states, regions, and districts require students to take one or more tests involving grammar and/or usage. The public is led to believe that these tests reveal student achievement in writing and language learning. Research, however, clearly shows that teaching traditional grammar alone does not help students write better, and may even be harmful to the development of effective writing skills by drawing time away from actual practice in composition. Further, research and theory suggest that students should probably not study formal grammar extensively until perhaps as late as the twelfth grade. Yet because of society's preoccupation with assessment, students receive yearly doses of grammar and usage to ensure they are prepared for these tests.

Certainly, some form of assessment is unavoidable in the interests of accountability. And if carried out with moderation and sophistication, assessment can help students learn and teachers teach. Therefore, we set down the following thoughts about assessment at all levels of education.

First, English teachers are the professionals most qualified to specify what is important in English studies: what are the understandings — and more important, the *ways of knowing and doing* — that our students should achieve. As professionals, we must insist that *at all levels* assessment should be based on our highest standards of learning rather than on mere memory.

In addition, we call for a study group of exemplary teachers and researchers from all levels of English studies to develop statements of goals that can serve as a basis for better assessment. The recent shift in the field of writing from multiple-choice tests to holistically scored tests of extended writing represents a move in the right direction. But it represents only a step, because even these holistic tests usually fail to allow for or measure certain skills that we hold as crucial in writing: sustained reflection before writing; exploratory prewriting; sharing drafts with peers for the sake of feedback and discussion; and revising on the basis of this social interaction.

Recently, some teachers and researchers have sought to find ways to test even these parts of the writing process. We need to insist on our highest goals in writing and thus encourage such continued exploration of new directions in testing.

In the area of reading and the study of literature, we badly need to state learning goals in ways that reflect the complex, highly constructive processes of reading, and that can serve as the basis for tests which enhance good teaching of reading and interpreting texts. At present, most tests undermine good teaching by stressing mere recognition or "decoding" and by implying that reading is a largely passive process of getting "right" answers.

Mass Testing

Mass testing programs — on school district, state, and national scales — need to be designed by teachers (with the help of experienced testers, but not under their direction) to be in harmony with the goals of the district programs. Moreover, a clear articulation of goals needs to precede the designing of any test. If a district decides to buy tests off the shelf, officials should be very careful that the goals of the test are appropriate (and if it is normed, these norms should be established on truly parallel students). Simplistic tests of information may be accurate in their own domain, but they deceive the public into thinking our goals ought to be simple. (One of the serious faults of the minimal essentials movement was that it rewarded teachers and students for avoiding complication or complexity.)

We commend several of the findings of the review committee of the National Academy of Education, which provided commentary on the report of the NAEP study group (see *The Nation's Report Card: Improving the Assessment of Student Achievement*):

- Assessment devices can and often do exert unhealthy influences on school curricula.

- Assessment devices must recognize the role of "instructional pluralism" by allowing classroom teachers the means for developing and organizing curriculum and instruction based on local needs and conditions.

- New types of activities and fewer time constraints in testing situations are necessary for measuring reading and writing skills in interactive classrooms.
- We must encourage, through the blending of research and pedagogical practice, new approaches to testing which will further improve learning.
- It can be misleading and dangerous to compare test results on a state-by-state, region-by-region, or school-by-school basis.

A Final Reminder

Lest we fall into thinking that assessment always necessitates the use of large, formal instruments, we should remember that the most trustworthy assessment is usually conducted by the individual teacher in his or her own classroom as an integral part of the teaching process. After all, a reliable and valid test is more likely to be possible when the activities or materials to be covered are discrete and sharply defined, as in a classroom. Sometimes one can test performance quite directly; in fact, most classroom activities test student skills and knowledge as part of the continuing efforts to improve. When any single measure is ineffective or insufficient at showing what the student really knows or can do, the ongoing teaching situation demands and inevitably brings forth a more successful measure in another mode.

Teacher Education and Professional Growth

The Carnegie Report, the Holmes Report, and many state reports on public schools point out that the pool of those who want to go into teaching is steadily shrinking. This fact is especially alarming given demographic data which suggest that we will need larger numbers of teachers beginning in 1990, and that societal and technological changes will make teachers' jobs much harder. Given these facts, it is necessary that we begin immediately to attract committed, creative, and intelligent people to the profession, as well as to encourage the gifted and able to remain in the profession.

Teacher Education

English and education units, programs, departments, and schools have a responsibility to work together to structure undergraduate teacher education programs to include:

1. systematic interaction among school professionals (teachers and administrators), education departments, and English departments in designing and monitoring such programs;
2. a judicious mix of learning theories, language theories, rhetorical/ writing theories, and literary/reading theories;
3. systematic observation of teaching at all levels of education for all teachers, K–graduate school; and
4. frequent opportunities to write, read, and speak — and to reflect on the nature of those processes.

Our professional organizations need to agree on more specific guidelines for education and English departments' collaboration on teacher education programs, including careful consideration of the place of ESL/EFL training in teacher education programs for all levels. The existing NCTE guidelines offer a useful basis for discussion.

Individuals, departments, institutions, and professional associations need to seek funding to:

1. build models of cooperation between practicing classroom teachers and teacher trainees in conjunction with colleges of education, English departments, and schools; and
2. support conferences, publications, and other work that makes explicit the intellectually rigorous and rich connections between learning theories, language theories, rhetorical theories, and literary theories, so that English and education departments better understand their mutual interest in learning and knowing through language and the potential of their collaboration/cooperation.

Graduate programs in English need to include courses, internships, and other programs which acknowledge that, among many other things, graduate programs are teacher education programs.

Those designing teacher education programs in English language arts must acknowledge the political constraints represented by state departments of education, certifying agencies, and assessments (e.g., the National Teachers Examination). These political constraints must be dealt with in the establishment of new, cooperative programs (English departments, colleges or departments of education, and public schools), because the ideals and goals of these programs can be undermined by external forces.

Professional Growth Opportunities

1. Opportunities for professional growth should include collaboration across levels (elementary, secondary, college), involvement of administrators as participants, and follow-up networking.

2. Professional organizations, school districts, and English and education departments should

- develop a range of models for providing teachers with support (time, money, recognition) to participate in professional growth activities
- seek funding for such programs
- educate the public about teachers' needs as professionals

Rights and Responsibilities of Students and Teachers

Preamble

In order to work productively, students and teachers in all subject areas should enjoy the following rights and privileges, which represent not luxuries but *necessary conditions* for effective learning and teaching. Because of the intensive student/teacher interaction in language arts classes, these conditions are particularly important to English teachers from elementary school through college. This list of rights covers all levels of education, although some items apply specifically to one institutional setting and not to others. The "responsibilities" in this list form the reverse side of the "rights." For example, the right of students to well-planned, productive classtime is a responsibility of teachers; the right of teachers to reciprocal evaluation is a responsibility to carry out such evaluation.

Rights of Students

Place

- A safe place to keep private possessions
- Safe and clean hallways, gymnasiums, and lunchrooms
- Sanitary bathrooms where doors are on stalls
- Private times
- Adequate public telephones to make personal phone calls at appropriate times
- Clean and cheerful classrooms
- A comfortable place to spend free time and to eat meals
- A well-equipped library, staffed by a professional librarian who also has training in learning
- An adequate supply of quality, up-to-date textbooks, resources, and materials

- Classroom libraries of quality literature
- Adequate food service

Time

- Times when teachers are available to meet with students
- Humane spacing of tests and homework
- Homework and assignments returned within a reasonable amount of time
- A reasonable, consistent, and public policy regarding absences, tardiness, and attendance
- Adequate time for breaks, including recess, lunch, and passing between classes
- Few or no classroom interruptions
- Classroom time that is planned and spent productively

Staff/Student Relations

- Substitute teachers who deal with students in a professional manner
- Teachers who are up-to-date on current teaching methods and their subject areas
- Teachers who treat students with a humane and caring attitude
- Administrators and counselors who are accessible to students and parents
- Teachers who make goals, expectations, and classroom guidelines clear from the beginning of the school year or semester
- Teachers who are not habitually late or absent
- A person to see (administrator, department head, counselor, ombudsperson, or community liaison) to appeal alleged unfair or abusive behavior
- Flexibility about use of language or dialect in journals or private writing or writing not directed to a specified audience
- Classrooms free of racial and sexual discrimination, especially including such discrimination in the setting of standards
- Teachers who are committed to students' personal as well as intellectual growth and who see students regularly

Rights of Teachers

Place

- A private classroom for elementary and secondary school; an appropriate classroom (size, configuration, equipment) for college
- Sufficient supplies of appropriate materials, including texts, to carry out the curriculum
- A private, comfortable place in which to meet with students, parents, or other teachers
- A place to be alone
- A safe place in which to keep private possessions
- A telephone in a department office or classroom, or any other arrangement that assures immediate and private contact with the outside world
- A clean, appealing lounge and private restrooms
- A large, up-to-date professional library
- An adequate number of functioning typewriters, word processors, copiers, and telecommunications equipment

Time

The items under this heading are primarily directed to elementary and secondary schools. Although some of these items are concerns at the college level, different circumstances pertain there.

- Some adjustable periods or segments in the school week for the purpose of meeting with students and parents
- Time for private planning (recommended: at least one hour every school day for K–12)
- Time each week during school for meeting and planning with other teachers (recommended: at least two hours each week for K–12)
- Time to be alone every school day
- A reasonable lunch period with no supervisory duties (recommended: forty-five uninterrupted minutes)
- Paid days to attend professional meetings and conferences
- An opportunity for teachers with outside professional duties and responsibilities — such as holding office in local, state, regional, national, and international groups — to engage in these activities without penalty

- Few or no classroom interruptions
- Sufficiently long class periods for the achievement of educational objectives
- No more than four classes per day with a maximum of 100 students at the secondary level; no more than twenty students for elementary teachers
- Opportunity to spend time with exemplary professionals and projects

Staff Status

- A decisive voice in the curriculum and all other matters that affect the teacher's professional life
- A voice in the hiring of new teachers in one's department
- Individual conferences with administrators, set at convenient and appropriate times, to discuss mutual concerns
- Evaluation only by persons with current knowledge about the learning and teaching of English
- Evaluation aimed at improving instruction rather than at judging the person
- Reciprocal evaluation: teachers evaluate all those who evaluate them
- Representation on the school board or board of trustees by a teacher elected by the faculty
- Regular, frequent provisions for growth and learning within the school
- A salary commensurate with the teacher's professional standing
- Opportunities for new teachers to be oriented by their colleagues to their new academic institution

College Writing Instructors

Many colleges currently employ large numbers of non-tenure-track and/or part-time instructors to teach writing, often at very low salaries and without fringe benefits or job security. These practices deny equity to the instructors involved, shortchange students, undermine efforts to establish writing as a legitimate enterprise in every college, and threaten the integrity of our institutions. The Coalition therefore endorses the spirit of the "Wyoming Resolution," reprinted here, and strongly supports the studies of this problem currently undertaken by the Conference on College Composition and Communication.

The Wyoming Conference Resolution

WHEREAS, the salaries and working conditions of post-secondary teachers with primary responsibility for the teaching of writing are fundamentally unfair as judged by any reasonable professional standards (e.g., unfair in excessive teaching loads, unreasonably large class sizes, salary inequities, lack of benefits and professional status, and barriers to professional advancement);

AND WHEREAS, as a consequence of these unreasonable working conditions, highly dedicated teachers are often frustrated in their desire to provide students the time and attention which students both deserve and need;

THEREFORE, BE IT RESOLVED that the Executive Committee of College Composition and Communication be charged with the following:

1. To formulate, after appropriate consultations with post-secondary teachers of writing, professional standards and expectations for salary levels and working conditions of post-secondary teachers of writing.

2. To establish a procedure for hearing grievances brought by post-secondary teachers of writing — either singly or collectively — against apparent institutional non-compliance with these standards and expectations.

3. To establish a procedure for acting upon a finding of non-compliance; specifically, to issue a letter of censure to an individual institution's administration, Board of Regents or Trustees, state legislators (where pertinent), and to publicize the finding to the public-at-large, the educational community in general, and to our membership.

Illustrations

Conference participants produced many more pages of commentary, position statements, and minutes than those recorded here. Visitors gave speeches. Other participants provided demonstrations. Although we have chosen to leave most of these materials in manuscript, we excerpt here a number of concrete illustrations of the problems and practices implied in the resolutions preceding this chapter. Statistical accounts of problems often do not mean much to nonteachers, especially in dramatizing the complicated interaction among difficult problems. Proposed solutions sometimes seem impracticable because they are not easily visualized. We have here selected a number of portraits and stories to address that need. To ensure privacy, we have altered some details, but we have retained the style of the originals — some starkly plain in suggesting the issues, some evocative as vignettes.

Teachers

First, we offer portraits of three composite teachers who are using methods approved by the secondary strand. These teachers emphasize questioning, writing in class, using multiple sources of information, working collaboratively in small groups, reading aloud, listening to one another. The teacher is a coach, a person who plans activities and suggests resources.

Miss Petrie

Miss Petrie smiles and indicates the pile of photocopied short stories on the small table. Each student who enters the class takes one, sits down to read, and then begins to write questions. A student new to the class is coached in the process by a "helper" who is self-appointed. While the students are thus occupied, Miss Petrie quietly calls up students to her desk singly, in pairs, in triads, depending on the topics which they have chosen and refined during the preceding two days. Each student has asked a series of questions about his or her topic. The first meeting with Miss Petrie is merely to discuss topics and

51

questions. Students listen to each other, or to Miss Petrie and themselves in the case of singles. The students return to their seats after the interview and finish their story questions. Then they decide on a mode of answering one question that they wish to deal with. The next total class activity will feature a group discussion based on the student-engendered questions on each story, and will help the class members to recall the questioning process, the kinds of questions asked, the varieties of responses, and the kinds of modes possible for further response. This discussion will also orient the new student. Options for further response include film, song, art, and various kinds of writing, among others.

Mr. Thompson

Mr. Thompson has put a poem, a short one, on the overhead projector. Students enter the class and cluster in circles to read the poem, perhaps reading it aloud for each other. Mr. Thompson reads the poem aloud for the whole class. Students write responses in their journals. Students are invited to share their responses with others in their clusters or anywhere in the room. Mr. Thompson identifies the poem as one written by a student the previous year and asks whether that fact would change any of their responses, and why or why not? A lively general discussion follows. Once again students return to their journals and pose questions engendered by the poem experience (not just the poem itself). Then they write on their inquiry cards (three-by-five lined cards) ideas engendered by the experience they wish to pursue ("research") during the rest of the two-hour time block. Mr. Thompson signs the cards, which constitute passes for students to use if they wish to go to the media center, the library, study carrels, or the VIP center (staffed by parent volunteers and occasionally, community persons) where students can contact "outside experts" in person or by phone. Students may want to write a poem in response, write their own essay versions, find other poems on the same subject, locate a poet who writes in this style or on this topic, question others about their responses to the poem, find out more about the poem, counsel students who have problems finding a line of pursuit, or simply talk with those who wish to discuss the project. Tomorrow, students will share their strategies with Mr. Thompson and each other. The actual project may take several days.

Dr. Valdez

Dr. Valdez has begun the drama section of his third-period class in American humanities. Since September students have been exploring theories which emerged from their small groups in history. They have completed oral and family histories, and examined bestselling books of the 1930s. They researched and wrote about what a typical American house would have looked like in the 1930s, written what the house might have "said." Then they looked at paintings, drama, and other topics researched and presented by small groups, using artifacts, documents, library books, etc. As the students apply this information in American humanities, one group works in the library on project planning and research, and other groups hold project conferences with Dr. Valdez in his office. At these conferences, students present their plans for study and feedback to the rest of the class. Jeff is painting in the style of Grant Wood, and Pat has researched ads for women's hats, noting how this style is typical of the decade.

Students

Here are members of a composite high school class and portraits of several individual college students. Together, they represent the wide diversity of backgrounds and aspirations our students bring to school. Although they are the voters of the future and they hope to share in our economic prosperity, many of them do not hear the messages of the traditional curriculum offered in lectures, assigned readings, and drills.

Janie

Janie lives with her mother, and both must work to be able to pay the rent and buy necessities. Janie is drifting through school. School seems much less interesting and relevant than her outside work. She has little or no time to do homework. The work assigned does not "speak" to her. She has no say in what she may study or pursue as a topic for research, reading, and writing. She is bored and discouraged.

Hugh

Hugh lives with his father. His mother died last year in an auto accident. His father is still grieving and is overwhelmed with trying to care for Hugh. Hugh was an honors student, but his work has slipped considerably. There is no one in school who can talk with him, find subjects to pursue that will help him to regain his interest in learning and his self-confidence as a learner. The English teacher who might have been able to meet Hugh's needs was transferred last year.

José

José is a very bright and earnest young man recently arrived from El Salvador. He is in transition from ESL classes. He wants to learn, to become a competent reader and writer in his new language. He patiently does his assigned work, but he confides to his counselor that he does not feel as if he is really learning how to use language. The drills and exercises that he does have outlived their usefulness. He needs more challenging, independent work that will help him in his new language situations. If he is not challenged, he may drop out.

Anna

Anna is a very quiet, introverted young woman. She is an above-average student, but she is seldom heard from in class. She submits very neat work and does everything she is assigned. But she is not developing any coping skills that will help her in the business career she hopes to pursue. She must be able to think and work independently, to speak and work collaboratively with others. Her English class, based on traditional reading, writing, and exercise activities, is not meeting the needs that she has, but does not recognize.

Philip

Philip is a "troublemaker." He has transferred through three schools already and is only in the first semester of the eleventh grade. He is intelligent, restless, angry. His needs have not been met. He is fascinated with cars. Once he helped to build a racing car with his uncle. If he could work at least part-time on projects which absorb him, he would be better able to discipline himself and stay out of trouble. He would acquire the skills in communication and cooperation necessary for him to be able to work as an apprentice.

Bret

Bret is a physically immature seventh grader, whose main interests are soccer and video games. When he returns home from school, he is expected to watch his younger brother until his parents arrive home at 5:00. He does not do homework because he thinks that his teachers assign chapters and exercises without much, if any, explanation. He doesn't understand the information in his history books and is always behind the rest of his English class because he is a slow reader. So he avoids reading, and instead watches MTV and plays video games. He is failing or getting Ds in most classes. He is afraid to acknowledge how far behind he is; he turns in very little written work. His parents are exasperated, bewildered, and angry with Bret because of his poor performance. They blame the school for his bad grades.

Yolanda

Yolanda is sixteen. She was pregnant at fifteen. The father was fourteen and went to another school. She no longer sees him. She lives with her mother, sisters, and brothers. Her mother works; a neighbor babysits. Yolanda is supported by welfare. She has to leave school to take the baby to a clinic when the baby is ill. Yolanda is too busy and too tired to do homework or much schoolwork. School has little meaning for her now. She wants to get a job. She probably will not stay in school for two more years in order to graduate.

Anton

Anton is fifteen. He loves clothes, cars, girls, sports. He is smart and articulate but is pulled away from school by outside pressures. His mother, who works and does not get home until 8:00 p.m., gives him money any time he needs it. He has much free time, frequently cuts school, is part of a fast crowd that loiters around neighborhood stores. He has been in trouble with the police and has been on probation. The gang probably is involved with drugs. For Anton, school is a world without meaning.

Michael

Michael is a curious and intelligent student. However, he has few organizational skills. When he begins a project, he reads many books and writes many drafts, but never completes assignments. He is a divergent thinker who explores the world and learns, but does not know how to pull his ideas together. Although he is the most intelligent student in the class, he gets Ds and Fs because his learning style does not conform to the system, and he is not getting any individual help.

Beldon

Beldon dropped out of school in the middle of his junior year. When asked why, he said that none of the reading meant anything to him or ever touched his life. It did not make any connection to the America which he knew and was led to believe in. He found nothing of his Chinese heritage, nothing about blacks or Hispanics whom he knew.

He felt alienated from the white, Euro-American curriculum that seemed to exclude him.

Happy Encounters

Here are two accounts of how college teachers have come to know and understand some of their nontraditional students.

Vince

The day after the first meeting of the senior seminar, Vince, a thin, bearded, twenty-eight-year-old, sauntered self-consciously into my office to discuss his project for the term. I had laid down only one requirement — that the students were to select a topic that deeply interested them. Vince fidgeted. His soft eyes stared at the floor. His first love, he said, was science fiction, but he thought that sci-fi was not a proper subject for his project, not really academic, not highly serious enough for a college course.

Vince, I discovered as we talked, had had little privilege. He was a veteran, married, the father of two young girls. He and his wife worked at a restaurant to support their family and pay his tuition, and he drove sixty miles each day to get back and forth to school. By his account, he had been raised by a hateful grandmother. To escape from her hounding presence, he'd turned to reading comic books. School provided no interest or challenge, though it was, he said, a respite from his grandmother's nagging. To escape from the boredom of his junior high, he'd read his comics in class, hiding them behind an open history or geography book. Comics — and later adventure stories — had hooked Vince into the world of pure romance. Aware of what it took to beat the system, Vince had squeaked through school, received his diploma, and, as one more way to escape from a dreary home life, enlisted in the army. Vince told me his story in his own Appalachian dialect, and I found myself wincing when he'd say "I seen" and "We done."

I asked what science fiction he'd read. "Arthur Clarke, Frank Herbert, Robert Silverberg, Ursula LeGuin." And then he ticked off a long list of writers I didn't know. He was not trying to impress. I'd asked a question about science fiction, and he assumed I knew enough about the subject to recognize his heroes and heroines — the authors in that large imaginative world into which he'd moved after leaving comics and macho adventures. He told me about the books he'd read since 1967, about the long reading list he'd compiled, about the extraordinary library he'd been able to amass from garage sales and sci-fi conventions (more than 4,000 books altogether), about his correspondence with Robert Silverberg, and about the sci-fi criticism he'd read ("most of it not very good"). He told me about discovering a water-stained copy of *Moby Dick* in a box of used books at a yard sale (he'd never heard of Melville), about how he couldn't put the book down and how he'd read it over and over in the meantime.

Before coming to my university, Vince had enrolled in a community college, where in his English survey course he'd discovered a whole new body of literature as compelling as his sci-fi stories. He was puzzled by the differences between the two kinds of writing, yet he felt that there was some common element in the sci-fi stories and the canonical texts that lay behind his appetite for narrative. This, it became clear as we talked, would be an issue that he might spend some time exploring. It was a question he wanted to ask, even though I nudged him a bit to get it to the surface. I suppose I was trying to get him to see that those things he felt deeply about were legitimate areas of inquiry and that he need not repress his love for sci-fi. And Vince did feel deeply about stories. He couldn't understand why other English majors he ran into would grumble about having to read their assignments in Sophocles and Faulkner. These things, he said, were dessert: He couldn't wait until he'd finished his homework in accounting so that he could enter the worlds of Oedipus and Ike McCaslin.

Vince completed his project, which I recommended for honors. His paper came directly from his own passionate encounter with books. His voice was honest, clear, eloquent. He'd found a topic he wanted to explore. Although his project began with direct experience, he was able to step back disinterestedly from that experience and to make his own meaning out of it. What Vince produced, in short, was the best piece of student writing I'd come upon in eighteen years of teaching.

Susan

She didn't look older than the traditional college student, but I knew that she was. She had the kind of intensity that characterizes students who are paying their own way, though I discovered later that she wasn't; that she was, in fact, the daughter of a well-known physician in the community and that she had dropped out and tuned out for several years. She never talked about it, except obliquely.

From the first day in English composition, I sensed her divided self: part of her was seduced by learning, part of her believed that she knew more than I could help her learn. But even the part that wanted to know, the part that stayed, was cynical. She liked to ask the "challenging" question and make the patronizing comment, couched, if she could, in the language of Akademic Kool.

"It appears that the thinking in this piece needs to be reexamined in the light of new insights into the psychology of dependency."

When the other members of the class said, in effect, "Whaaaat?" she seemed surprised. Everyone, she implied, knew that. Or ought to. She almost never missed class.

Each student in class was keeping a journal of observations, the kind others could read "for profit." When Susan came in for her first writing conference, she brought her journal for me to look at. I had looked forward to reading it, because she had been writing some interesting things in class, although her voice was still more Akademic Kool than it was Susan. I was surprised, then, to find that her journal contained writing that was not only sporadic, but empty. The journal had not been a useful activity for her.

We talked about it, and she put down the idea of keeping the journal.

"I think we did this assignment in the third or fourth grade." Kool. But by this time, I knew that statements like that were self-defense, not arrogance. I knew, too, that I wanted more than anything to see this student experience the sharp pleasure of insight. If I asked her to keep her entries, to be patient with herself and the process, she might be even more determined to prove the task worthless.

I decided to set her free and suggested that she stop writing in her journal. Because I thought she would interpret this as a victory, I was unprepared for the passion of her response. She sat up in one movement, then slid to the edge of the chair. She wanted to be sure she had understood me, so I repeated my suggestion, and I was just a little anxious when she enunciated slowly in a sandpaper voice: "YOU . . . SHOULD . . . MAKE . . . ME . . . DO . . . IT!"

Fumbling for words, I tried to explain that we had been making ourselves more aware of how we wrote, what helped us and what got in our way. At this time, the journal was getting in her way, and there was no stone tablet anywhere that said: Thou must keep a journal in order to be a writer.

I didn't think I had done a good job of it. Susan had not given me to understand that she approved or even understood, and I felt the rest of the semester that somehow she held against me what she perceived as my weakness. I never knew whether or not she ever discovered the joys of her own mind or her own voice. I thought long and hard about the moment in the conference, and even accumulated an array of imagined scenarios which would have been the beginning of self-confidence for her, rather than the replication of betrayal. But I still catalogued Susan under "failure."

A couple of years later, I happened to be in the Galleria, a shopping center in town, when a young woman came scurrying toward me, calling my name: "Dr. A! Dr. A!" It was Susan. It was as if we were back in that messy office on that fall day. She would be stunned if she knew I had thought so much about her, I thought.

Well, maybe she wouldn't. After the required amenities, the first thing she said to me was: "You know what? I'm keeping a journal — and I love it."

Sometimes — but only sometimes — our failures may not be failures.

Vignettes and Anecdotes

Finally, here are some vignettes and anecdotes that comment on how our educational system works, how schools and teachers have had to reconceptualize their own roles in the lives of such schools. A number of these anecdotes demonstrate changes in institutional structure or teaching method, made in response to changing student populations.

Time

Having asked students to do a paper out of class after developing several in class, I was expecting even stronger papers than previously, because I thought students would have had more time to work on them. My expectations were not met. When I asked students why they thought that was, they told me it was because they had more time to work in silence and concentrate on their writing when they worked in class. These freshman writing students supported each other in saying that they never had fifty uninterrupted minutes for work outside the classroom.

The "Right" Meaning

One day a student came to my office and announced she was looking for the previous occupant, who had been her English teacher two years ago. I informed her that he was no longer in the department (he hadn't received tenure), and she looked at me with evident despair. I asked her what was the matter, and she explained: "Professor X taught us this story in his class [I forget the name of the story], and he told us what it meant, and now I have the same story in another class and I've forgotten what its interpretation is. I need to find him so he'll tell me, because this other teacher won't."

She asked me if I knew the story, and she was a bit disgusted when I didn't. I told her that she should try to think for herself about what the story might mean, but this lame advice clearly demonstrated to her that the wrong person had been fired.

The Teacher-Consultant

I can say without qualification that last year was the most stressful, painful, hurtful, debilitating year of my life. Many of my days were wrapped in blackness. One day — this day I am remembering — I was unable to create a face to "meet the faces that we meet" — and I called the office and asked someone to post a note in my class, saying that I could not attend class that day but would be there the next day. It was the only day I had missed that year, and I spent a bit of time feeling guilty for leaving my class in the lurch.

How little I had learned about how I — and my class — had changed.

When I arrived the next day, I walked toward the classroom, concentrating on what I would say about my absence. I should have known better. The day before, the students had arrived, had *not* found the secretary's note, had waited a few minutes, and then held class. "Gee," they said, "you missed a great class yesterday, but we assigned Erin to take notes for you — and Gary taped the last thirty minutes. Hey — where were you, anyway?"

Ten years ago, my class would have waited ten or fifteen minutes and then left. What has changed? Me, my classroom, and my course organization. My theory of learning. *The locus of control.* And that, as Frost says, has made all the difference.

The Trusting Administrator

It was nearly time for the second semester in our new high school. I still had nothing but the title of the course I had been assigned to teach, "Poetry and Drama." There were no curriculum guides, no books, no department teachers even to tell me. And I was the department chairman!

Suddenly the custodian brought me some textbooks, but he couldn't recall where he found them — textbooks on teaching poetry and drama as an oral interpretation course.

With less than a week left, I pleaded my case with our principal. "I'm not prepared to teach oral interpretation — and I don't want to. And the books just came!"

He smiled. "Well, what *do* you want to teach?"

Here was my chance.

"American humanities," I said. "I've been waiting to do this for ten years."

"OK," he said.

I rushed home, designed the interdisciplinary course, ordered the paperbacks (to come in time), and began a new life as a teacher. Here was a principal who trusted me and broke all the rules.

(*P.S.*: I taught all four of his kids in American humanities.)

A Ghost School

Ethan Middle School opened for grades 5–8 in the fall of 1970. It wasn't quite finished yet. The cafeteria and gym weren't open; we had to have brown-bag lunches in the resource center and phys ed in the halls. There were still openings in the building, so mice came in and ate our lunches as they sat on the shelves. But none of this mattered. We were a group committed, enthusiastic, and eager to begin life as a middle school.

Much preparation had come before — preparation for community and staff. Those of us who eagerly embraced the concept of the middle school (and that was most of the teachers) had not only had time to meet together to plan, but also to visit the middle school on which ours was modeled. The program and population were similar, and both communities could afford to provide an excellent facility with appropriate support staff, equipment, and materials. We read books and journals about what a middle school should be and were committed to providing a model program.

The building was actually designed with four "houses" (or pods) constructed around the resource center and fine-arts rooms, with the gym and cafeteria attached at the back. Each house contained twelve classrooms, four small conference rooms connected to classrooms (with glass windows for observation from the classrooms), two science prep rooms in each house . . . In addition, there was an auditorium, a large group instruction room, and several small conference rooms for faculty. In other words, we had a flexible facility which would accommodate a variety of instructional strategies and organizations.

Teachers of math, science, social studies, and language arts were assigned to interdisciplinary teams, and each team of four teachers was assigned 100 students for a four-and-one-half-hour block of time daily. There was no "master schedule," no bells, no defined class periods. Instead, four professionals were given the responsibility for planning, structuring, and monitoring the learning of 100 students. This team concept guaranteed that the students had a sense of belonging to a group; the teachers, who had one-and-one-half hours of planning time together each day, actually planned each day's schedule based on the needs of each subject at that time. They knew the students well, met collectively with the parents as they came in for conference, and often met as a group with a child.

Monitoring the teaching/learning were two deans (the school design was intended to have four, one in each house) who were facilitators for teaching, not evaluators and program imposers. In fact, as they often met daily with the teams, they participated in curriculum development, helped to provide resources, and were liaisons between the team and the administration and community.

The curriculum itself was developed and continually changed by the team teachers who wrote interdisciplinary units. A central theme or question (power, emerging nations, science fiction, brotherhood, fact or fiction) served as the foundation for the units, and the skills of each discipline were built into them. As teachers developed these units (often working nights and weekends at one another's homes without complaining!) a sense of cooperation and collegiality developed, and as teams continued to work together, there was a strong bond and sense of pride between teachers.

Flexibility was the key. On Monday, the language arts teacher may have wanted to show a film, so instead of showing it four times to four classes, it could be scheduled for a single large-group viewing, with pre- and post-viewing activities shared by all four teachers. This then meant that one of the other disciplines could have longer classes; or all could. If the science teacher wanted double lab periods, they could be built in. Tests in math could be given at once by all four teachers. There was time for sustained silent reading and writing every day. We could group, regroup, and subgroup for different purposes, and often had students in both heterogeneous and homogeneous groups in a single day. If one teacher needed to see a particular small group of students, it could be arranged. Teachers cotaught, learned as they observed one another teach, and learned respect for one another's skills in a setting which is not possible in a typical junior or senior high school. (In the traditional setting, it is possible never to observe another teacher teaching.)

There was an incredible environment of enthusiasm, sharing, and ownership in the middle school. Teachers did feel empowered to make decisions and create curriculum. There was nothing laissez faire about it; we planned a detailed schedule for the following week each Friday, but by mid-week we evaluated our progress and made changes if needed. We were able to have frequent guest speakers, field trips, and even our own team concert series because we *could* schedule it. Most units lasted three to four weeks, and sometimes we would build in a one- or two-week "break" between units for catching up or prepping for a standardized test. But even then, our schedule changed daily. At least once a year we planned a unit which would totally eliminate subject divisions, with each teacher doing the same things. The science fiction unit of my own team was an example. Students spent one intensive week of building four ecosystems. In all classes they read, discussed, researched, planned, and built. The four teachers were simply advisors and resources. Students planned the schedule, set the rules, and determined the evaluative criteria. By the end of the week, the four classrooms had been transformed into four independent habitats for survival.

By 1980, however, the community climate had changed. "Back to Basics" had hit, and several disgruntled teachers who chose not to work so hard and who wanted the privacy and inflexibility of a fixed, no-team schedule had been making their unhappiness known to school board members. The principal was promoted from the middle school to central administration, and the death knell was sounded. The interim principal and the new superintendent were very unhappy, because they did not understand the principles on which the school was organized. The philosophy sounded too student-oriented (not enough painful learning and structure) and, worst of all, they could not understand the many schedules turned in on Friday by the twelve teams. Surely, they decided, learning could not be going on in such an unstructured environment. Student scores would definitely rise if we returned to what we had been — a little high school.

And so we did. We are now departmentalized and have eight periods a day. Students move around the school for their classes; teachers have little time to know students and no common planning time with other teachers to discuss students, curriculum, parents, or professionalism. Teachers feel no sense of ownership or pride in their program and resent the supervision and structure that are both inflexible and depersonalized. Permanent walls have been erected in the double classrooms, small-group rooms have become storage closets, and homogeneous grouping exists in at least half of the school schedule. Instead of having a supportive group of four teachers who work together, who monitor the students' progress together, alert one another to problems and concerns about individual students, and brainstorm solutions, the child has four teachers (actually eight, counting the fine and applied arts) who may not even see one another for weeks at a time (there are three lunch periods, too).

In other words, all of those characteristics that created a personalized, supportive environment for children and an enthusiastic ownership for teachers have been eliminated. Fifth graders are now treated like high school seniors. We have made it possible for a child to be a "cypher" in the school — to be unknown and unnoticed. A nonperson. That is how many of the teachers who taught in the "real" middle school feel.

We have gone from . . .	to . . .
A sense of community	A sense of competition
Personalization	Depersonalization
Flexibility	Inflexibility
Integrated curriculum	Fragmented curriculum
Student-centered	Subject-centered
Teacher involvement	Teacher passivity
Learning-centered	Grade-centered
Collegiality	Isolation

Laura

May 8, 1987

We celebrate Mother's Day in our first-grade classroom this Friday afternoon. The children perform a play for their mothers entitled "The Big Race" — the story of the tortoise and the hare. Laura is the "turtle" who wins the race.

A few minutes later Laura reads aloud the book she has authored about her mother. The group laughs as she reads about learning to count with her cousins when she was three years old. Laura writes: "I was learning six. Then my Mom came in and asked what we were doing. I said, 'I'm learning sex!' " Laura's mother is delighted. The reading continues with a hilarious account of a family squabble between mom and dad over a broken plate. Laura concludes the anecdote, "So then I just went in and watched TV." Laura looks at me and smiles as she pauses, waiting for her audience to quiet before she goes on. I wink at her; I know she is thinking, "Wait till they hear the next part. It's the funniest of all." She reads about a llama spitting in mom's eye on a visit to the zoo. Laura's way with words has brought delight to everyone. I remember a week earlier when Laura and I sat to type her draft and she said, "This is the best part. I put it last so that everyone will feel happy at the end."

May 9, 1987

Saturday night, around 11:45 p.m., a light bulb ignites fabric in a closet outside Laura's bedroom. Laura wakes. She cannot get through the flames, and by the time firefighters reach her it is too late. Laura dies. No one else is injured.

May 11, 1987

The children and I gather on our Sharing Rug in the classroom. I have no plans. We start to talk. There are endless interruptions until Michael says, "Mrs. Alston, can we shut the door so people stop bothering us?" So Michael shuts the door. "Are you going to read us the newspapers?" they ask. "Is that what you'd like?" "Yes," comes the unanimous response. The children huddle close; a dozen knees nuzzle against me. I read aloud the four-paragraph story on the front page of the *Sunday News* that accompanies a picture of our Laura sprawled on the lawn of her home with firefighters working over her. I read the longer story in Monday morning's paper, which carries Laura's school picture. We cry. We talk and cry some more. And then we read Laura's books — writing which Laura determined was her best throughout the year and which was "published" to become part of our classroom library. These books are stories of Laura and her family, stories with titles such as *My Dad Had a Birthday* and *When My Grandmother Came to My House*. Laura's voice comes through loud and clear with its sense of humor and enthusiasm. We laugh and enjoy her words. "Laura was a good writer," they say. "She always makes us laugh when we read her stories." Then Dustin says, "You know, it feels like Laura is right here with us, right now. We just can't see her."

A short time later we begin our writing workshop. Every child chooses to write about Laura this day. Some write about the fire, some memories of Laura as a friend. I write with them. After forty-five minutes it is time to go to art and there are cries of disappointment at having to stop. We will come back to the writing. There will be plenty of time. The last five weeks of school will be filled with memories of Laura as we work through our loss together. The children will decide to leave her desk in its place in the room because, "It's not in our way and anyway, this is still Laura's room even if she's not really here anymore." Laura's mother and little brother will come in to see us. On the last day they will bring us garden roses that Laura would have brought. Laura will always be a part of us, and none of us will ever be the same.

In the days immediately following Laura's death and in the weeks since then, certain thoughts have been rattling around in my head: I'm so glad that I teach the way I do. I'm so glad I really knew Laura. I know that I can never again teach in a way that is not focused on children. I can never again put a textbook or a "program" between me and the children. I'm glad I knew Laura so well. I'm glad all of us knew her so well. I'm glad the classroom context allowed her to read real books, to write about real events and experiences in her life, to share herself with us and to become part of us and we of her. I'm grateful for a classroom community that nurtured us all throughout the year and especially when Laura was gone. Laura left a legacy. Part of that legacy is the six little published books and the five-inch thick stack of paper that is her writing from our daily writing workshops. When we read her words, we hear again her voice and her laughter.

Appendix A

Participants

All of the participants were chosen as leaders by the elected officers of one or more of the sponsors, but the organizations tried to sample the variety of a large field. The coalition decided that elementary and secondary school perspectives had to be represented substantially by teachers active in those schools. They also sought from within their large memberships (some 100,000 teachers) people known for work in linguistics, media, speech communication, literary theory, writing, traditional literary criticism, popular culture, textbook and tradebook writing, minority literatures, education, cognitive theory, and other subfields of interest. Finally, they tried to represent social groups of the country — racial, ethnic, geographic, economic — as well as patterns of public and private schooling at all levels. As the conference began, probably not more than a half dozen people, including the conference planners, had even met personally as many as half of the participants, and most people knew only a very few others. The alphabetical list of participants is included below. Each name is identified according to whether the person sat with the elementary (E), secondary (S), or college (C) subgroups.

Name and Strand	Affiliations
Gwendolyn Alexander (S)	Calvin Coolidge High School, Washington, D.C. (NCTE)
Bruce C. Appleby (C)	Southern Illinois University (CEE)
*Paul B. Armstrong (C)	University of Oregon (MLA)
Carol Avery (E)	Nathan C. Schaeffer Elementary School, Lancaster, Pa. (NCTE)
Rosalinda Barrera (E)	New Mexico State University at Las Cruces (NCTE)
Rudine Sims Bishop (E)	Ohio State University (NCTE)
*Wayne Booth (S)	University of Chicago (MLA)

John G. Bordie (C)	University of Texas at Austin (MLA)
Craig Bowman (S)	Alameda Junior High School, Lakewood, Colo. (NCTE)
Nancy Broz (S)	William H. Allen III Middle School, Moorestown, N.J. (NCTE)
Marie Buncombe (C)	Brooklyn College (CLA)
*Frederick R. Burton (E)	Barrington Elementary School, Columbus, Ohio (NCTE)
Donna Carrara (E)	Montclair Kimberly Academy, Montclair, N.J. (NCTE)
*Candy Carter (S)	Tahoe Truckee High School, Truckee, Calif. (NCTE)
*Jane Christensen (S)	Deputy Executive Director (NCTE)
Katherine Cummings (C)	University of Washington (MLA)
*Robert Denham (S)	Director (ADE)
Angela G. Dorenkamp (C)	Assumption College (CEA)
Richard Dunn (C)	University of Washington (MLA)
*Carole Edmonds (C)	Kellogg Community College (ADE)
Peter Elbow (C)	University of Massachusetts at Amherst (MLA)
Janet Emig (S)	Rutgers University (NCTE)
*Phyllis Franklin (C)	Executive Director (MLA)
Alice Gasque (C)	University of South Dakota (ADE)
Jeffrey Golub (S)	Shorecrest High School, Seattle, Wash. (NCTE)
*Michael Halloran (C)	Rensselaer Polytechnic Institute (CCCC)
Charles Harris (C)	Illinois State University (ADE)
Joan Hartman (C)	College of Staten Island (ADE)
Betsy S. Hilbert (C)	Miami Dade Community College
Janie Hydrick (E)	MacArthur Elementary School, Mesa, Ariz. (NCTE)
Julie M. Jensen (E)	University of Texas at Austin (NCTE)

Larry Johannessen (S)	Lyons Township High School, LaGrange, Ill. (NCTE)
Tom Jones (S)	Wyoming Valley West High School, Plymouth, Pa. (CSSEDC)
*John Joyce (C)	Nazareth College of Rochester (CEA)
Mary M. Kitagawa (E)	Richey Elementary School, Tucson, Ariz. (NCTE)
Mary Krogness (E)	Shaker Heights Elementary School, Shaker Heights, Ohio (NCTE)
*Richard Lloyd-Jones (S)	University of Iowa (NCTE)
Joe Lostracco (C)	Austin Community College (NCTE)
*Andrea Lunsford (C)	Ohio State University (MLA)
*John C. Maxwell (E)	Executive Director (NCTE)
Kathleen A. McCormick (C)	Carnegie-Mellon University (MLA)
Nancy McHugh (S)	Grant High School, Van Nuys, Calif. (NCTE)
Nellie McKay (C)	University of Wisconsin (MLA)
Vera E. Milz (E)	Way Elementary School, Bloomfield Hills, Mich. (NCTE)
Diane T. Orchard (E)	Lapeer Community Schools, Mich. (NCTE)
Jane E. Peterson (C)	Richland Community College (CCCC)
Rosentene B. Purnell (C)	California State University (CCCC)
Robert Scholes (C)	Brown University (MLA)
Faith Schullstrom (E)	Guilderland Central School District, Guilderland, N.Y. (CEE)
*George B. Shea (S)	Belleville West High School, Belleville, Ill. (NCTE)
Susan Stires (E)	Boothbay Region Junior High School, Boothbay Harbor, Maine (NCTE)
Peggy Swoger (S)	Mountain Brook Junior High School, Birmingham, Ala. (NCTE)

William Teale (E)	University of Texas at San Antonio (NCTE)
*Eleanor Q. Tignor (C)	LaGuardia Community College (CLA)
Joseph I. Tsujimoto (S)	Punahou School, Honolulu, Hawaii (NCTE)
Gregory L. Ulmer (C)	University of Florida (MLA)
Gary F. Waller (C)	Carnegie-Mellon University (MLA)
Jerry W. Ward, Jr. (C)	Tougaloo College (MLA)
Brooke Workman (S)	West High School, Iowa City, Iowa (NCTE)

* = Assisted with this report

Sally Parry, an MLA staff member who served as conference coordinator, handled the logistical needs of the conference and contributed to it informally.

Appendix B

After the Urbana meeting of English Coalition representatives, the separate organizations agreed to keep their current representatives in place to plan the conference, although some others were added. Many of these people eventually were also present at the conference: Bruce Appleby, Nancy Broz, Jane Christensen, Robert Denham, Richard Dunn, Phyllis Franklin, Alice Gasque, Charles Harris, John Joyce, Richard Lloyd-Jones, John Maxwell, Rosentene Purnell, Faith Schullstrom, and Eleanor Q. Tignor. Some of the original planners were unable to attend: James E. Miller (University of Chicago), Thelma Curl (Norfolk State University), J. F. Kobler (North Texas State University), Maxine Hairston (University of Texas at Austin), and Erika Lindemann (University of North Carolina at Chapel Hill). At various times, detailed planning and proposal writing were turned over to Phyllis Franklin, John Maxwell, Jane Christensen, Richard Lloyd-Jones, and Charles Harris. During the conference itself, the full committee was augmented by people who were at that time serving as chairs or recorders for the subgroups, as well as by others who volunteered to help; but Phyllis Franklin, John Maxwell, Jane Christensen, Robert Denham, and Charles Harris handled most of the immediate details of keeping the participants on the tasks. Sally Parry — before, during, and after the conference — handled most of the logistical arrangements.

Condensed Diary of Conference Events

The conference plan called for four general phases of deliberation: a review of changed conditions for teaching, identification of goals for teaching, description of methods for accomplishing the goals, and a review of systems for developing teachers. Before the conference, participants were asked to read as much as possible from a list of books and articles, and to prepare a position statement on a subtopic drawn from the four areas for deliberation. These statements and a brief biographical note on each participant were distributed to the group. Although several noted specialists were invited to speak to the group, most of the sessions simply took advantage of the expert knowledge of those who were members of the group. Word processors and photocopying equipment made communications among the group members relatively simple and abundant.

July 6, 1987

Arrival, registration. After the opening dinner, a plenary session for welcomes and an explanation of the history and goals of the conference by Phyllis Franklin (MLA), John Maxwell (NCTE), Eleanor Q. Tignor (CLA), and John Joyce (CEA).

July 7 and 8, 1987

The opening phase of the conference was devoted to identifying changes in students, curricula, school environment, and community and institutional contexts during the last ten or fifteen years. The opening plenary session was devoted to an address, "Literature vs. Literacy," by Chester E. Finn, Jr., assistant secretary for research and improvement, U.S. Department of Education. Conference participants then divided into three groups to discuss the issues outlined for Part One of the conference, the address by Mr. Finn, and the relevant position papers on the subject by the participants themselves.

During the morning the group was divided into "A strands," concentrating their attention on elementary, secondary, and college programs. The members of these strands are identified in Appendix A. During the afternoon, groups were rearranged into "B strands," systematically mixing the participants. The B strand groups were rearranged again each week of the conference, and later the morning and afternoon pattern was also revised. Each small group had its own leader and recorder, new people each week. They reported the substance of their discussions to a plenary session on July 8.

July 9 to 12, 1987

The second phase of the conference was devoted to identifying general goals for student achievement in language and writing, as well as in the study of literature, other texts, and general cultural literacy. Jerome Singer, professor of psychology and director of the Clinical Psychology Program at Yale University, spoke at a plenary session on "Developing Imagination and Literacy: The Role of Early Family Influences and Television." E. D. Hirsch, Jr., professor of English at the University of Virginia, also spoke to a plenary session on cultural literacy generally and discussed his book on the subject. The "strand workshops" picked up these themes, especially in conjunction with their own position papers. Minutes of the smaller meetings were copied and distributed to members of each group and to others who wanted them, but the summary reports were still offered in a general session during the evening of July 11. Additional position papers were written and circulated for discussion in the groups.

July 13 to 21, 1987

The third phase of the conference was devoted to determining how the goals identified in earlier discussions might be realized. Three days were devoted each to the study of language, the study of writing, and the study of literature and other texts, particularly considering classroom practices, curricula, and selection of materials. Speakers at plenary sessions were Shirley Brice Heath, professor of English and linguistics, Stanford University, "Developing Language Skills"; Richard Lloyd-Jones, professor of English, University of Iowa, "The Goodly Fellowship of Writers and Readers"; and Gerald Graff, professor of English, Northwestern University, who discussed the role of critical theory in the study of English.

Janet Emig, professor of English education, Rutgers University, conducted a plenary demonstration on learning theories; Nellie McKay, professor of American and Afro-American literature, University of Wisconsin, led a model graduate literature seminar on a text by a black woman author; Wayne Booth, professor of English, University of Chicago, conducted a model class discussion of a metaphysical poem; Robert Scholes, professor of English, Brown University, gave a close reading of a basal reader and demonstrated the teaching of poetic techniques; Brooke Workman, teacher at West High School (Iowa City, Iowa), conducted a demonstration of teaching a short story in a high school environment; and William Teale, professor of education, University of Texas at San Antonio, gave a reading and commentary on a literary text for children.

The strand workshops continued meeting about four hours a day, but the plenary sessions for reports were discontinued in favor of a circulation of written minutes and informal discussions at meals and elsewhere.

July 22 to 24, 1987

The final phase of the conference was devoted to considering the implications of the previous discussions for the training of teachers and to adopting resolutions outlining the views of the group in consensus. There were no formal speakers, but there were frequent plenary sessions and a constant flow of new documents. The resolutions appearing in this book were approved unanimously or with one or two dissenting votes. Two people and an advisory committee were appointed to edit the resolutions and to supply general reference information about the conference as background for the book to be written by Peter Elbow.

Appendix C

Although each person at the conference began with substantial professional training and experience, a common reading list was circulated during the spring to help focus issues. The list of "Selected Readings" here is shortened, but includes a few additions suggested later by participants. In particular, we have added a bibliography in learning theory prepared by Janet Emig (Appendix D) because of the importance such studies assumed in the discussions. In addition, each person received a brief professional sketch of the other participants, and each prepared a statement about some aspect of English teaching today, a group of statements that roughly followed the plan and general topics of the conference.

Historical Change, Contemporary Influences, and Public Expectations

Applebee, Arthur. 1974. *Tradition and Reform in the Teaching of English: A History.* Urbana, Ill.: National Council of Teachers of English.

Bloom, Alan. 1987. *The Closing of the American Mind.* New York: Simon and Schuster.

Boyer, Ernest L. 1983. *High School: A Report on Secondary Education in America.* New York: Harper and Row.

Dewey, John. 1916. *Democracy and Education.* New York: Macmillan.

———. 1979. *Experience and Education.* New York: Collier Books.

Doyle, Walter. 1986. Academic Work. In *Academic Work and Educational Excellence: Raising Student Productivity,* edited by Tommy M. Tomlinson and Herbert J. Walberg, 175–95. Berkeley, Calif.: McCutchan.

Goodlad, John I. 1984. *A Place Called School: Prospects for the Future.* New York: McGraw-Hill.

Graff, Gerald. 1987. *Professing English.* Chicago: University of Chicago Press.

Hirsch, E. D., Jr. 1987. *Cultural Literacy: What Every American Needs to Know.* Boston: Houghton Mifflin.

Holbrook, Hilary Taylor. 1984. Qualities of Effective Writing Programs. *ERIC Digest.* Urbana, Ill.: ERIC Clearinghouse.

King, David C., and Sharon Flitterman-King. 1986. The Tug-of-War Is on between Writing Approaches: Emphasis on Process Challenges the Five-Paragraph Essay. *ASCD Curriculum Update,* December: 1–8.

National Commission on Excellence in Education. 1984. *A Nation at Risk: The Imperative for Educational Reform. A Report to the Nation and the Secretary of Education.* Washington, D.C.: U.S. Government Printing Office.

Postman, Neil. 1985. *Amusing Ourselves to Death.* New York: Viking.

Sanacore, Joseph. 1985. Six Reading Comprehension Myths. *Educational Leadership,* February: 43–47.

Shugrue, Michael. 1985. Project English and Beyond. *ADE Bulletin* 80:18–21.

Smitherman-Donaldson, Geneva. 1987. Opinion: Toward a National Public Policy on Language. *College English* 49:29–36.

Our Students: Who Are They? / Goals and Measurements of Success

Applebee, Arthur N., Judith A. Langer, and Ina V. S. Mullis. 1986. *The Writing Report Card: Writing Achievements in American Schools.* Princeton: National Assessment of Educational Progress (Educational Testing Service).

Ascher, Carol. 1984. *Black Students and Private Schooling.* Trends and Issues Series #4. New York: ERIC Clearinghouse.

Kanagawa, Hiro. 1986. Student Talk: Please Don't Think Me Disrespectful . . . *Middlebury Alumni Magazine,* Autumn: 14–15.

Lunsford, Andrea A. 1979. Cognitive Development and the Basic Writer. *College English* 41:38–47. Reprinted in *The Writing Teacher's Sourcebook,* edited by E. P. J. Corbett and Gary Tate, 257–68. New York: Oxford University Press, 1981.

Zimiles, Herbert. 1986. The Changing American Child. In *Academic Work and Educational Excellence: Raising Student Productivity,* edited by Tommy M. Tomlinson and Herbert J. Walberg, 61–84. Berkeley, Calif.: McCutchan.

The Classroom: Teaching Practices and Training, Curriculum, and Resources

Bruner, Jerome. 1986. *Actual Minds, Possible Worlds.* Cambridge: Harvard University Press.

Calkins, Lucy. 1983. *Lessons from a Child: On the Teaching and Learning of Writing.* Portsmouth, N.H.: Heinemann.

Csikszentmihalyi, Mihalyi. 1982. Intrinsic Motivation and Effective Teaching: A Flow Analysis. In *New Directions for Teaching and Learning: Motivating Professors to Teach Effectively,* edited by J. Bess, 15–26. San Francisco: Jossey-Bass.

Csikszentmihalyi, Mihalyi, and Jane McCormack. 1986. The Influence of Teachers. *Phi Delta Kappan* 68:415–19.

Cuban, Larry. 1986. Persistent Instruction: Another Look at Constancy in the Classroom. *Phi Delta Kappan* 68:7–11.

Elbow, Peter. 1986. *Embracing Contraries.* New York: Oxford University Press.

Fancher, Robert T. 1984. English Teaching and Humane Culture. In *Against Mediocrity: The Humanities in America's High Schools,* edited by Chester E. Finn, Jr., Diane Ravitch, and Robert T. Fancher, 49–69. New York: Holmes and Meier.

Fillion, Bryant. 1983. Let Me See You Learn. *Language Arts* 60:702–10.

Fortune, Ron. 1986. Introduction. *School–College, Collaborative Programs in English.* New York: Modern Language Association.

Gardner, Howard. 1983. *Frames of Mind: The Theory of Multiple Intelligences.* New York: Basic Books.

Hahn, Amos L., and Ruth Garner. 1985. Synthesis of Research on Students' Ability to Summarize Text. *Educational Leadership,* February: 52–55.

Heath, Shirley Brice. 1983. *Ways with Words: Language, Life, and Work in Communities and Classrooms.* Cambridge: Cambridge University Press.

Hillocks, George, Jr. 1984. What Works in Teaching Composition: A Meta-analysis of Experimental Treatment Studies. *American Journal of Education* 93:133–70.

Postman, Neil. 1979. *Teaching as a Conserving Activity.* New York: Delacorte.

Singer, J. L., and D. G. Singer. 1981. Television and Reading in the Development of the Imagination. *Children's Literature* 9:126–36.

————. 1983. Psychologists Look at Television: Cognitive, Developmental, Personality, and Social Policy Implications. *American Psychologist* 7:826–34.

Sizer, Theodore. 1984. *Horace's Compromise: The Dilemma of the American High School.* Boston: Houghton Mifflin.

Vygotsky, L. S. 1978. *Mind in Society: The Development of Higher Psychological Processes.* Edited by M. Cole, et al. Cambridge: Harvard University Press.

Literacy: Reading, Literature, and Interpretation

Barth, John. 1985. Writing: Can It Be Taught? *New York Times Book Review,* June 16: 1+.

Booth, Wayne. 1979. *Critical Understanding.* Chicago: University of Chicago Press.

Culler, Jonathan. 1981. *The Pursuit of Signs: Semiotics, Literature, Deconstruction.* Ithaca: Cornell University Press.

Eagleton, Terry. 1983. *Literary Theory.* Minneapolis: University of Minnesota Press.

Flynn, Elizabeth A., and Patrocinio Schweickart. 1986. *Gender and Reading.* Baltimore: Johns Hopkins University Press.

Fort, Keith. 1975. Form, Authority, and the Critical Essay. In *Contemporary Rhetoric: A Conceptual Background with Readings,* edited by W. Ross Winterowd, 171–83. New York: Harcourt.

Goelman, Hillel, Antoinette Oberg, and Frank Smith. 1985. *Awakening to Literacy.* Portsmouth, N.H.: Heinemann.

Lipking, Lawrence. 1981. Literacy Criticism. In *Introduction to Scholarship in Modern Languages and Literatures*, edited by Joseph Gibaldi, 79–97. New York: Modern Language Association.

Mailloux, Steven. 1979. Learning to Read: Interpretation and Reader Response Criticism. *Studies in the Literary Imagination*, Spring. Reprinted in *American Critics at Work*, edited by Victor Kramer. Troy, N.Y.: Whitston Publishers, 1985.

———. 1982. *Interpretive Conventions: The Reader in the Study of American Fiction*. Ithaca: Cornell University Press.

Scholes, Robert. 1986. *Textual Power.* New Haven: Yale University Press.

Showalter, Elaine, editor. 1985. *The New Feminist Criticism.* New York: Pantheon.

Smith, Frank. 1983. Reading Like a Writer. *Language Arts*, May.

White, Edward. 1986. *Teachers and the Teaching of Writing.* San Francisco: Jossey-Bass.

Literacy: The Study and Generation of Language

Applebee, Arthur. 1986. Problems in Process Approaches: Toward a Reconceptualization of Process Instruction. In *The Teaching of Writing: Eighty-fifth Yearbook of the National Society for the Study of Education, Part II*, edited by Anthony R. Petrosky and David Bartholomae. Chicago: University of Chicago Press.

Calkins, Lucy. 1985. *The Art of Teaching Writing.* Portsmouth, N.H.: Heinemann.

Elbow, Peter. 1985. The Shifting Relationships between Speech and Writing. *College Composition and Communication* 36:282–303.

Emig, Janet. 1977. Writing as a Mode of Learning. *College Composition and Communication* 28:122–27.

Hansen, Jane, Thomas Newkirk, and Donald Graves. 1985. *Breaking Ground: Teachers Relate Reading and Writing in the Elementary School.* Portsmouth, N.H.: Heinemann.

Hillocks, George. 1984. What Works in Teaching Composition. *American Journal of Education* 93:133–70.

———. 1986. *Research on Written Composition.* Urbana, Ill.: National Council of Teachers of English.

Ong, Walter. 1978. Literacy and Orality in Our Times. *ADE Bulletin* 58:1–7.

Pattison, Robert. 1982. *On Literacy.* New York: Oxford University Press.

Sanacore, Joseph. 1985. Six Reading Comprehension Myths. *Educational Leadership*, February: 43–47.

Tate, Gary, editor. 1987. *Teaching Composition: Twelve Bibliographical Essays.* Fort Worth: Texas Christian University Press.

Appendix D

Learning Theories and Literacy: Readings Selected by Janet Emig

Bannister, David. 1980. *The Inquiring Man: The Psychology of Personal Constructs.* Malabar, Fla.: Krieger.

Battaglini, D. W., and R. Schenkat. 1987. Fostering Cognitive Development in College Students — The Perry and Toulmin Models. *ERIC Digest.*

Bloom, Benjamin S. 1956. *Taxonomy of Educational Objectives.* New York: David McKay.

Boden, Margaret. 1980. *Jean Piaget.* New York: Viking.

Bruner, Jerome. 1973. The Role of Tutoring. In *The Relevance of Education.* New York: Norton.

———. 1986. *Actual Minds, Possible Worlds.* Cambridge: Harvard University Press.

Dewey, John. 1938. *Education and Experience.* New York: Macmillan.

———.1956. *The Child and the Curriculum, the School and Society.* Chicago: University of Chicago Press.

Donaldson, Margaret. 1978. *Children's Minds.* New York: Norton.

Emig, Janet. 1983. Non-Magical Thinking. In *The Web of Meaning.* Upper Montclair, N.J.: Boynton/Cook.

Freire, Paulo. 1981. *Pedagogy of the Oppressed.* New York: Continuum.

Gagne, Robert. 1977. *The Condition of Learning.* New York: Holt, Rinehart, and Winston.

Gardner, Howard. 1973. *Quest for Mind: Piaget, Lévi-Strauss, and the Structuralist Movement.* New York: Knopf.

———.1983. *Frames of Mind: A Theory of Multiple Intelligences.* New York: Basic Books.

Gilligan, Carol. 1982. *In a Different Voice: Psychological Theory and Women's Development.* Cambridge: Harvard University Press.

John-Steiner, Vera. 1985. *Notebooks of the Mind: Explorations of Thinking.* Albuquerque: University of New Mexico Press.

Kelly, George. 1963. *A Theory of Personality: The Psychology of Personal Constructs.* New York: Norton.

Kohlberg, Lawrence. 1981. *Philosophy of Moral Development: Moral Stages and the Idea of Justice.* San Francisco: Harper and Row.

Langer, Susanne. 1967. *Mind: An Essay on Human Feeling.* Baltimore: Johns Hopkins University Press.

Luria, Aleksandr. 1966. *Higher Critical Functions in Man.* New York: Basic Books.

———. 1968. *Speech and the Development of Mental Processes in the Child.* London: Staples Press.

Mead, George Herbert. 1967. *Mind, Self and Society: From the Standpoint of a Social Behaviorist.* Chicago: University of Chicago Press.

Parker, Robert P., and Vera Goodkin. 1987. *The Consequences of Writing: Enhancing Learning in the Disciplines.* Upper Montclair, N.J.: Boynton/Cook.

Perry, William G. 1970. *Forms of Intellectual and Ethical Development in the College Years.* New York: Holt, Rinehart, and Winston.

Piaget, Jean. 1977. *The Essential Piaget.* Edited by Howard Gruber. New York: Basic Books.

Polanyi, Michael. 1958. *Personal Knowledge.* London: Routledge and Paul.

———. 1975. *Meaning.* Chicago: University of Chicago Press.

Polya, George. 1945. *How to Solve It: A New Aspect of Mathematical Method.* Princeton: Princeton University Press.

Rosaldo, Michelle. 1980. *Knowledge and Passion: Ilongot Notions of Self and Social Life.* New York: Cambridge University Press.

Vygotsky, Lev. 1962. *Thought and Language.* Cambridge: MIT Press.

Wertsch, James. 1985. *Vygotsky and The Social Formation of Mind.* Cambridge: Harvard University Press.

Appendix E

In August 1984, leaders of the Coalition of English Associations met at NCTE headquarters in Urbana, Illinois. Among other activities, the coalition created a statement called "Some Plain Truths about Teaching English," designed to speak to the neglect of English studies in a variety of reform reports current at the time. The coalition urged a broader definition of English and stressed the importance of studying literature. It advocated smaller classes for language learning, cautioned the public about overemphasis on mass testing, and insisted that English teachers at all levels must have more support and encouragement to improve their performance. The text of the report is as follows.

Some Plain Truths about Teaching English

Prompted by recent reports on American education, many communities are now trying to strengthen their schools' English programs as a part of general educational reform. A number of government agencies are considering proposals which will affect the teaching of English. But without a clear understanding of the field, the reformers may fail to achieve this goal. The reports offer little specific guidance to those who must implement the changes. Some of the reports simply assert the value of English; others offer suggestions based on limited understanding of the subject. To provide a foundation for successful reform, we offer the public, as a preliminary response, a few plain truths:

1. *English studies include the study of both literature and writing.*
   Although most of the reports assert the value of learning to write, they fail to recognize the importance of studying literature.
   The ability to write effectively is obviously crucial. Writing helps people conduct the business of living. It helps them solve problems and express themselves. It forces them to create meaning in words, to explore who they are and what they think. Writing provides an invaluable means of understanding all fields and of sharing knowledge.

The study of literature is equally important. Literature enriches and broadens the experience of life. It plays a significant role in learning to use language well. By studying literature, people learn how ideas, emotions, and moral commitments have been fused in language. By learning to analyze and interpret the language of literature they learn to deal with ambiguity and to remain wary of answers that close off the possibility of discussion. Learning how to interpret complex, emotionally intense literary works enables them to improve their own writing and helps them interpret the various forms of communication they encounter in their daily lives.

Learning to interpret literature is a key link between functional literacy and the highest intellectual purposes of learning.

2. *So much excellent literature exists that different schools may reasonably make different selections of literature for their students.*

Many reports raise the question of what students should read. A number suggest the importance of establishing a common body of literature.

Students should read works that help them define and understand their own values and experiences and those of others. All students should read widely in the literatures from their own cultures and regions, from the pluralistic American experience, and from the world at large.

3. *Small classes are necessary for effective language learning.*

While some reports call for better teaching, few acknowledge the need for small English classes.

Students learn effective writing and critical reading best through practice. When they write, they need frequent opportunities to go over their work with classmates and teachers. When they read, they must have enough time to discuss literature with the teacher individually or in small groups. To promote learning, teachers must respond to individual variations in their students' development. Effective language learning requires coaching by mature, well-educated teachers. Such coaching requires small classes.

4. *Achievement in English cannot be evaluated adequately by mass testing.*

Many of the reports accept data from mass testing programs as justification for their recommendations.

Some achievements may be partially measured by mass testing. But the use of language is a complex activity; it can be evaluated only by frequent observation of real performances of reading and writing.

Teaching and learning are also complex activities that cannot be evaluated simplistically. Even test publishers explicitly warn against misusing test scores as measures of effective programs, courses, or teachers. Relying on mass testing inevitably leads to programs oriented toward test scores rather than educational goals.

5. *Teachers must have support to continue their growth as professionals.* Some reports point out that communication among English teachers across grade levels and institutions remains inadequate, but few reports suggest remedies.

Overcoming the isolation of teachers requires that they have more time and additional opportunities to discuss their work with colleagues and to continue their studies. Although professional organizations strive to provide adequate forums, teachers need more encouragement and support from their administrators and communities to participate in such forums in their pursuit of excellence in teaching.

As representatives of national associations of those who study and teach English, we welcome the dialogue now taking place among parents, educators, and community leaders. We invite responses to this statement and intend to prepare more extensive explanations of these principles and others of concern to the public and the profession. We see these exchanges as opportunities to work together and to enhance the quality of instruction we offer our students.

Among the reports on education reform referred to by the Coalition of English Associations are the following:

- *A Nation at Risk: The Imperative for Educational Reform*
- *Educating Americans for the 21st Century*
- *Report of the Twentieth Century Fund Task Force on Federal Elementary and Secondary Education Policy*
- *Action for Excellence: A Comprehensive Plan to Improve Our Nation's Schools*
- *Meeting the Need for Quality: Action in the South*
- *Academic Preparation for College: What Students Need to Know and Be Able to Do*
- *The Paideia Proposal*

- *High School: A Report on Secondary Education in America*
- *America's Competitive Challenge: The Need for a National Response*
- *A Place Called School: Prospects for the Future*

Participants

People attending the meeting of the Coalition of English Associations, August 3–5, 1984, at the National Council of Teachers of English headquarters, 1111 Kenyon Road, Urbana, Illinois, are listed below.

- For the Modern Language Association: Executive Director English Showalter
- For the Association of Departments of English: President James E. Miller, Jr. (chair, Department of English, University of Chicago), who presided at the sessions; ADE Director Phyllis Franklin; and President-elect Charles B. Harris (chairperson, Department of English, Illinois State University)
- For the National Council of Teachers of English: Vice President Richard Lloyd-Jones (chair of English and director, School of Letters, University of Iowa); Secondary Section Chair Skip Nicholson (teacher, South Pasadena Senior High School, California); Executive Director John C. Maxwell; and Associate Executive Director Jane Christensen
- For the Conference on College Composition and Communication: National Chair Rosentene B. Purnell (professor and director, PAS Writing Program, California State University, Northridge) and CCCC Executive Committee Member Erika Lindemann (associate professor of English and director of composition, University of North Carolina)
- For the College Language Association: Past President Eleanor Q. Tignor (associate professor of English, LaGuardia Community College, Long Island City, New York) and CLA Liaison Thelma Curl (assistant dean, School of Arts and Letters, Norfolk State University, Virginia)
- For the College English Association: Executive Secretary John J. Joyce (chair, Department of English, Nazareth College of Rochester, New York) and Vice President J. F. Kobler (professor of English, North Texas State University)

Appendix F

English Coalition Conference Theme: Democracy through Language

The English Coalition believes that language arts instruction can and should make an indispensable contribution to educating students for participation in democracy, because:

1. the interactive classroom necessary for learning how to write and read fosters development of the abilities to communicate, to listen, and to think critically — in the classroom and beyond;
2. the multiplicity of ways in which language can be read and written encourages students to appreciate different perspectives and to articulate their own points of view;
3. the great variety in the subject matter of humanities instruction facilitates an understanding of cultural diversity.

These assumptions rest on three related strands of argument:

1. *Research in Learning Theory*

   Current psychological research supports the view that learning takes place most effectively in an interactive setting where students are encouraged to develop and test hypotheses on their own. Such classrooms focus on what students already know in order to build on it. Active exchange with other students and the teacher is crucial for making learning an integral part of the student's experience. The subject matter is important not only for its own sake, but also as a way of developing transferable abilities in writing, reading, and thinking.

2. *Changes in Society*

   Language arts instruction is especially important in a heterogeneous, post-industrial society. In an age when the membership of the community is becoming more and more linguistically, culturally, and socially diverse, an interactive classroom focusing on each student individually is a practical necessity, because students no longer conform to a single type. The increased heterogeneity of our society also gives new urgency to enhancing students' ability to appreciate cultural diversity and multiple ways of reading and writing. The information explosion makes learning how to read and write absolutely vital for living, because without these abilities students will not be able to assimilate, evaluate, and control the immense amount of knowledge and the great number of messages which are produced every day. The development of new media similarly requires of citizens an enhanced ability to use different ways of reading and writing, and language arts instruction has an important role to play here as well.

3. *Democracy and Language Arts*

Citizens of a democracy must be able to appreciate diversity even as they advocate their own beliefs about what is good and true. Teaching students how and why different ways of reading can find different meanings in the same text can provide important experience in understanding and appreciating opposing perspectives. Learning about the many different kinds of writing and ways of thinking which are the subject matter of the language arts curriculum can expand the capacity of students to imagine and value worlds other than their own. The ability to communicate their views in oral and written form and to listen with comprehension to the views of others is also indispensable to citizens in a democracy, and enhancing this ability is a major aim of language arts education.

Editors

Richard Lloyd-Jones is professor of English at the University of Iowa and a member of NCTE's editorial board. He is a past president of NCTE, past chair of CCCC, past director of ADE, and past chair of the MLA division on the teaching of writing. He is coauthor of *Research in Written Composition* and codesigner of Primary Trait Scoring. Lloyd-Jones received the ADE Francis Andrew March Award for service to the profession and the Iowa Council of Teachers of English Distinguished Service Award.

Andrea A. Lunsford is professor and vice chair for rhetoric and composition at The Ohio State University. A former teacher of middle school, high school, and community college students, she has authored articles in numerous periodicals and books. The coauthor of four books — *A Preface to Critical Reading* with Richard Altick; *Essays in Classical Rhetoric and Modern Discourse* with Robert Connors and Lisa Ede; *Four Worlds of Writing* with Janice Lauer, Gene Montague, and Janet Emig; and *The St. Martin's Handbook* with Robert Connors — she is completing a study of collaborative writing. Lunsford is the 1989 chair of the Conference on College Composition and Communication.

DATE DUE

DEC 15 1997			

DEMCO 38-297